BY BERTRAND RUSSELL

1903	*The Principles of Mathematics*
1910	*Philosophical Essays*
1914	*Our Knowledge of the External World*
1916	*Principles of Social Reconstruction*
1917	*Political Ideals*
1918	*Roads to Freedom*
1918	*Mysticism and Logic*
1919	*Introduction to Mathematical Philosophy*
1920	*The Practice and Theory of Bolshevism*
1921	*The Analysis of Mind*
1923	*The Prospects of Industrial Civilization* (with Dora Russell)
1925	*The ABC of Relativity*
1925	*On Education*
1927	*Outline of Philosophy*
1928	*Sceptical Essays*
1929	*Marriage and Morals*
1930	*The Conquest of Happiness*
1932	*Education and Social Order*
1934	*Freedom and Organization: 1814-1914*
1935	*In Praise of Idleness*
1938	*Power*
1940	*An Inquiry into Meaning and Truth*
1945	*History of Western Philosophy*
1948	*Human Knowledge*
1949	*Authority and the Individual*
1950	*Unpopular Essays*
1952	*The Impact of Science on Society*
1954	*Human Society in Ethics and Politics*
1956	*Logic and Knowledge*
1956	*Portraits from Memory*
1957	*Why I am Not a Christian* (ed by Paul Edwards)
1958	*Bertrand Russell's Best* (ed by Robert Egner)
1959	*My Philosophical Development*
1961	*Fact and Fiction*
1967	*The Autobiography of Bertrand Russell Vol. 1*
1968	*The Autobiography of Bertrand Russell Vol. 2*
1969	*The Autobiography of Bertrand Russell Vol. 3*
1972	*The Collected Stories*
1975	*Mortals and Others* (ed by Henry Ruja)
1983	*The Collected Papers of Bertrand Russell Vol. 1*
1984	*The Collected Papers of Bertrand Russell Vol. 7*
1985	*The Collected Papers of Bertrand Russell Vol. 12*
1986	*The Collected Papers of Bertrand Russell Vol. 8*
1987	*The Collected Papers of Bertrand Russell Vol. 9*

PHILOSOPHICAL ESSAYS

ESSAYS

BERTRAND RUSSELL

London and New York

First published in 1910.
Published in 1966 by George Allen & Unwin.
First published in the United States of America in 1967
by Simon & Schuster.

Paperback edtion first published in 1994 by
by Routledge
11 New Fetter Lane, London EC4P 4EE

Simultaneously published in the USA and Canada
by Routledge
29 West 35th Street, New York, NY 10001

British Library Cataloguing in Publication Data

A CIP catalogue record is available from the British Library.

Library of Congress Cataloging in Publication Data

Also available.

ISBN 0–415–10579–X

CONTENTS

PREFACE

The volume to which this is a preface is essentially a reprint of a book, with the same title, published in 1910. However, two essays in that volume, namely 'The Free Man's Worship' and 'The Study of Mathematics', were reprinted in 'Mysticism and Logic' and are therefore not included in the present volume. They are replaced by an article on history and one on Poincaré's 'Science and Hypothesis'.

I have not attempted to make such emendations in the texts reprinted in this volume as might be called for by changes in my opinions during the intervening fifty-five years. The chief change is that I no longer believe in objective ethical values as I did when (following Moore) I wrote the first essay in the present volume.

PREFACE TO ORIGINAL EDITION

The following essays, with the exception of the last, are reprints, with some alterations, of articles which have appeared in various periodicals. The first three essays are concerned with ethical subjects, while the last four are concerned with the nature of truth. I include among the ethical essays the one on 'The Study of Mathematics', because this essay is concerned rather with the *value* of mathematics than with an attempt to state what mathematics is. Of the four essays which are concerned with Truth, two deal with Pragmatism, whose chief novelty is a new definition of 'truth'. One deals with the conception of truth advocated by those philosophers who are more or less affiliated to Hegel, while the last endeavours to set forth briefly, without technicalities, the view of truth which commends itself to the author. All the essays, with the possible exception of the one on 'The Monistic Theory of Truth', are designed to appeal to those who take an interest in philosophical questions without having had a professional training in philosophy.

I have to thank the editor of *The New Quarterly* for permission to reprint 'The Study of Mathematics' and Sections I, II, III, V and VI of the essay on 'The Elements of Ethics', and for Section IV I have to thank the editor of the *Hibbert Journal*. My acknowledgments are also due to the editors of *The Independent Review*, *The Edinburgh Review*, *The Albany Review*, and the *Proceedings of the Aristotelian Society*, for permission to reprint the essays II, IV, V and VI respectively. In the sixth essay as originally printed, there was a third section, which is now replaced by the seventh essay.

OXFORD
July 1910

Postscript.—The death of William James, which occurred when the printing of this book was already far advanced, makes me wish to express, what in the course of controversial writings does not adequately appear, the profound respect and personal esteem which I felt for him, as did all who knew him, and my deep sense of the public and private loss occasioned by his death. For readers trained in philosophy, no such assurance was required; but for those unaccustomed to the tone of a subject in which agreement is necessarily rarer than esteem, it seemed desirable to record what to others would be a matter of course.

October 1910

PHILOSOPHICAL ESSAYS

I

THE ELEMENTS OF ETHICS[1]

I. THE SUBJECT-MATTER OF ETHICS

1. The study of Ethics is perhaps most commonly conceived as being concerned with the questions 'What sort of actions ought men to perform?' and 'What sort of actions ought men to avoid?' It is conceived, that is to say, as dealing with human conduct, and as deciding what is virtuous and what vicious among the kinds of conduct between which, in practice, people are called upon to choose. Owing to this view of the province of ethics, it is sometimes regarded as *the* practical study, to which all others may be opposed as theoretical; the good and the true are sometimes spoken of as independent kingdoms, the former belonging to ethics, while the latter belongs to the sciences.

This view, however, is doubly defective. In the first place, it overlooks the fact that the object of ethics, by its own account, is to discover true propositions about virtuous and vicious conduct, and that these are just as much a part of truth as true propositions about oxygen or the multiplication table. The aim is, not practice, but propositions about practice; and propositions about practice are not themselves practical, any more than propositions about gases are gaseous. One might as well maintain that botany is vegetable or zoology animal. Thus the study of ethics is not something

---

[1] What follows is largely based on Mr G. E. Moore's *Principia Ethica*, to which the reader is referred for fuller discussions. Sections I and II of the following essay are reprinted from the *New Quarterly*, February 1910; section III from the *New Quarterly*, May 1910; section IV from the *Hibbert Journal*, October 1908; and sections V and VI from the *New Quarterly*, September 1910.

outside science and co-ordinate with it: it is merely one among sciences.

2. In the second place, the view in question unduly limits the province of ethics. When we are told that actions of certain kinds ought to be performed or avoided, as, for example, that we ought to speak the truth, or that we ought not to steal, we may always legitimately ask for a reason, and this reason will always be concerned, not only with the actions themselves, but also with the goodness or badness of the consequences likely to follow from such actions. We shall be told that truth-speaking generates mutual confidence, cements friendships, facilitates the dispatch of business, and hence increases the wealth of the society which practises it, and so on. If we ask why we should aim at increasing mutual confidence, or cementing friendships, we may be told that obviously these things are good, or that they lead to happiness, and happiness is good. If we still ask why, the plain man will probably feel irritation, and will reply that he does not know. His irritation is due to the conflict of two feelings—the one, that whatever is true must have a reason; the other, that the reason he has already given is so obvious that it is merely contentious to demand a reason for the reason. In the second of these feelings he may be right; in the first, he is certainly wrong. In ordinary life, people only ask *why* when they are unconvinced. If a reason is given which they do not doubt, they are satisfied. Hence, when they do ask *why*, they usually have a logical right to expect an answer, and they come to think that a belief for which no reason can be given is an unreasonable belief. But in this they are mistaken, as they would soon discover if their habit of asking *why* were more persistent.

It is the business of the philosopher to ask for reasons as long as reasons can legitimately be demanded, and to register the propositions which give the most ultimate reasons that are attainable. Since a proposition can only be proved by means of other propositions, it is obvious that not all propositions can be proved, for proofs can only begin by assuming something. And since the consequences have no more certainty than their premises, the things that are proved are no more certain than the things that are accepted merely because they are obvious, and are then made the basis of our proofs. Thus in the case of ethics, we must ask why such and such actions ought to be performed, and continue our backward inquiry for reasons until we reach the kind of proposition of which proof is impossible, because it is so simple or so obvious that nothing more fundamental can be found from which to deduce it.

3. Now when we ask for the reasons in favour of the actions which moralists recommend, these reasons are, usually, that the consequences of the actions are likely to be *good*, or if not wholly good, at least the best possible under the circumstances. Hence all questions of conduct presuppose the decision as to what things other than conduct are *good* and what *bad*. What is called good conduct is conduct which is a means to other things which are good on their own account; and hence the study of what is good on its own account is necessary before we can decide upon rules of conduct. And the study of what is good or bad on its own account must be included in ethics, which thus ceases to be concerned only with human conduct.

The first step in ethics, therefore, is to be quite clear as to what we mean by good and bad. Only then can we return to conduct, and ask how right conduct is related to the production of goods and the avoidance of evils. In this, as in all philosophical inquiries, after a preliminary analysis of complex data we proceed again to build up complex things from their simpler constituents, starting from ideas which we understand though we cannot define them, and from premisses which we know though we cannot prove them. The appearance of dogmatism in this procedure is deceptive, for the premises are such as ordinary reasoning unconsciously assumes, and there is less real dogmatism in believing them after a critical scrutiny than in employing them implicitly without examination.

II. THE MEANING OF GOOD AND BAD

4. Good and Bad, in the sense in which the words are here intended (which is, I believe, their usual sense), are ideas which everybody, or almost everybody, possesses. These ideas are apparently among those which form the simplest constituents of our more complex ideas, and are therefore incapable of being analysed or built up out of other simpler ideas. When people ask 'What do you mean by "good"?' the answer must consist, not in a verbal definition such as could be given if one were asked 'What do you mean by "pentagon"?' but in such a characterization as shall call up the appropriate idea to the mind of the questioner. This characterization may, and probably will, itself contain the idea of good, which would be a fault in a definition, but is harmless when our purpose is merely to stimulate the imagination to the production of the idea which is intended. It is in this way that children are taught the names of colours: they are shown (say) a red book, and told that that is red; and for fear they should think 'red' means 'book', they are shown also a red flower, a red ball, and so on, and told that these are all red. Thus the idea of redness is conveyed to their minds, although it is quite impossible to analyse redness or to find constituents which compose it.

In the case of 'good', the process is more difficult, both because goodness is not perceived by the senses, like redness, and because there is less agreement as to the things that are good than as to the things that are red. This is perhaps one reason that has led people to think that the notion of good could be analysed into some other notion, such as pleasure or object of desire. A second reason, probably more potent, is the common confusion that makes people think they cannot understand an idea unless they can define it—forgetting that ideas are defined by other ideas, which must be already understood if the definition is to convey any meaning. When people begin to philosophize, they seem to make a point of forgetting everything familiar and ordinary; otherwise their acquaintance with redness or any other colour might show them how an idea can be intelligible where definition, in the sense of analysis, is impossible.

5. To explain what we mean by Good and Bad, we may say that a thing is good when on its own account it ought to exist, and bad when on its own account it ought not to exist. If it seems to be in our power to cause a thing to exist or not to exist, we ought to try to make it exist if it is good, and not exist if it is bad. When a thing is good, it is fitting that we should feel pleasure in its existence; when it is bad, it is fitting that we should feel pain in its existence. But all such characterizations really presuppose the notions of good and bad, and are therefore useful only as means of calling up the right ideas, not as logical definitions.

It might be thought that 'good' could be defined as the quality of whatever we ought to try to produce. This would merely put *ought* in the place of *good* as our ultimate undefined notion; but as a matter of fact the good is much wider than what we ought to try to produce. There is no reason to doubt that some of the lost tragedies of Aeschylus were good, but we ought not to try to re-write them, because we should certainly fail. What we ought to do, in fact, is limited by our powers and opportunities, whereas the good is subject to no such limitation. And our knowledge of goods is confined to the things we have experienced or can imagine; but presumably there are many goods of which we human beings have absolutely no knowledge, because they do not come within the very restricted range of our thoughts and feelings. Such goods are still goods, although human conduct can have no reference to them. Thus the notion of good is wider and more fundamental than any notion concerned with conduct; we use the notion of good in explaining what right conduct is, but we do not use the notion of right conduct in explaining what good is.

6. A fairly plausible view is that 'good' means the same as 'desired', so that when we say a thing is good we mean that it is desired. Thus anything is good which we either hope to

acquire or fear to lose. Yet it is commonly admitted that there are bad desires; and when people speak of bad desires, they seem to mean desires for what is bad. For example, when one man desires another man's pain, it is obvious that what is desired is not good but bad. But the supporter of the view that 'good' means 'desired' will say that nothing is good or bad in itself, but is good for one person and perhaps bad for another. This must happen, he will say, in every case of a conflict of desires; if I desire your suffering, then your suffering is good for me, though it is bad for you. But the sense of *good* and *bad* which is needed in ethics is not in this way personal; and it is quite essential, in the study of ethics, to realize that there is an impersonal sense. In this sense, when a thing is good, it ought to exist on its own account, not on account of its consequences, nor yet of who is going to enjoy it. We cannot maintain that for me a thing ought to exist on its own account, while for you it ought not; that would merely mean that one of us is mistaken, since in fact everything either ought to exist or ought not. Thus the fact that one man's desire may be another man's aversion proves that 'good', in the sense relevant to ethics, does not mean the same as 'desired', since everything is in itself either good or not good, and cannot be at once good for me and bad for you. This could only mean that its effects on me were good, and on you bad; but here good and bad are again impersonal.

7. There is another line of argument, more subtle but more instructive, by which we can refute those who say that 'good' means 'desired', or who propose any other idea, such as pleasure, as the actual *meaning* of 'good'. This line of argument will not prove that the things that are good are not the same as the things that are desired; but it will prove that, if this were the case, it could not be proved by appealing to the *meaning* of the word 'good'. So far, it might be thought that such an argument could only have a purely logical importance. But in fact this is not so. Many ethical theories have been based upon the contention that 'good' means so-and-so, and people have accepted consequences of this contention which, if they

had relied upon inspection untrammelled by false theory, they would almost certainly have rejected. Whoever believes that 'good' means 'desired' will try to explain away the cases where it seems as if what is desired is bad; but if he no longer holds this theory, he will be able to allow free play to his unbiased ethical perceptions, and will thus escape errors into which he would otherwise have fallen.

The argument in question is this: If anyone affirms that the good is the desired, we consider what he says, and either assent or dissent; but in any case our assent or dissent is decided by considering what the good and the desired really are. When, on the contrary, someone gives a definition of the meaning of a word, our state of mind is quite different. If we are told 'a pentagon is a figure which has five sides', we do not consider what we know about pentagons, and then agree or disagree; we accept this as the meaning of the word, and we know that we are getting information, not about pentagons, but merely about the *word* 'pentagon'. What we are told is the sort of thing that we expect dictionaries to tell us. But when we are told that the good is the desired, we feel at once that we are being told something of philosophical importance, something which has ethical consequences, something which it is quite beyond the scope of a dictionary to tell us. The reason of this is, that we already know what we mean by the good, and what we mean by the desired; and if these two meanings always applied to the same objects, that would not be a verbal definition, but an important truth. The analogue of such a proposition is not the above definition of a pentagon, but rather: 'A pentagon (defined as above) is a figure which has five angles.' Whenever a proposed definition sets us thinking whether it is true in fact, and not whether that is how the word is used, there is reason to suspect that we are not dealing with a definition, but with a significant proposition, in which the word professedly defined has a meaning already known to us, either as simple or as defined in some other way. By applying this test, we shall easily convince ourselves that all hitherto suggested definitions of the good are significant, not merely verbal, propositions; and that therefore, though they *may* be true in fact, they do not give the meaning of the word 'good'.

The importance of this result is that so many ethical theories depend upon the denial of it. Some have contended that 'good' means 'desired', others that 'good' means 'pleasure', others again that it means 'conformity to Nature' or 'obedience to the will of God'. The mere fact that so many different and incompatible definitions have been proposed is evidence against any of them being really definitions; there have never been two incompatible definitions of the word 'pentagon'. None of the above are really definitions; they are all to be understood as substantial affirmations concerning the things that are good. All of them are, in my opinion, mistaken in fact as well as in form, but I shall not here undertake to refute them severally.

8. It is important to realize that when we say a thing is good in itself, and not merely as a means, we attribute to the thing a property which it either has or does not have, quite independently of our opinion on the subject, or of our wishes or other people's. Most men are inclined to agree with Hamlet: 'There is nothing good or bad but thinking makes it so.' It is supposed that ethical preferences are a mere matter of taste, and that if X thinks A is a good thing, and Y thinks it is a bad thing, all we can say is that A is good for X and bad for Y. This view is rendered plausible by the divergence of opinion as to what is good and bad, and by the difficulty of finding arguments to persuade people who differ from us in such a question. But the difficulty in discovering the truth does not prove that there is no truth to be discovered. If X says A is good, and Y says A is bad, one of them must be mistaken, though it may be impossible to discover which. If this were not the case, there would be no difference of opinion between them. If, in asserting that A is good, X meant merely to assert that A had a certain relation to himself, say of pleasing his taste in some way; and if Y, in saying that A is not good, meant merely to deny that A had

a like relation to himself: then there would be no subject of debate between them. It would be absurd, if X said 'I am eating a pigeon-pie', for Y to answer 'that is false: I am eating nothing'. But this is no more absurd than a dispute as to what is good, if, when we say A is good, we mean merely to affirm a relation of A to ourselves. When Christians assert that God is good, they do not mean merely that the contemplation of God rouses certain emotions in them: they may admit that this contemplation rouses no such emotion in the devils who believe and tremble, but the absence of such emotions is one of the things that make devils bad. As a matter of fact, we consider some tastes better than others: we do not hold merely that some tastes are ours and other tastes are other people's. We do not even always consider our own tastes the best: we may prefer bridge to poetry, but think it better to prefer poetry to bridge. And when Christians affirm that a world created by a good God must be a good world, they do not mean that it must be to their taste, for often it is by no means to their taste, but they use its goodness to argue that it *ought* to be to their taste. And they do not mean merely that it is to God's taste: for that would have been equally the case if God had not been good. Thus, *good* and *bad* are qualities which belong to objects independently of our opinions, just as much as *round* and *square* do; and when two people differ as to whether a thing is good, only one of them can be right, though it may be very hard to know which is right.

9. One very important consequence of the indefinability of 'good' must be emphasized, namely, the fact that knowledge as to what things exist, have existed, or will exist, can throw absolutely no light upon the question as to what things are good. There might, as far as mere logic goes, be some general proposition to the effect 'whatever exists, is good', or 'whatever exists, is bad', or 'what will exist is better (or worse) than what does exist'. But no such general proposition can be proved by considering the *meaning* of 'good', and no such general proposition can be arrived at empirically from experience, since we do not know the whole of what does

exist, nor yet of what has existed or will exist. We cannot therefore arrive at such a general proposition, unless it is itself self-evident, or follows from some self-evident proposition, which must (to warrant the consequence) be of the same general kind. But as a matter of fact, there is, so far as I can discover, no self-evident proposition as to the goodness or badness of all that exists or has existed or will exist. It follows that, from the fact that the existent world is of such and such a nature, nothing can be inferred as to what things are good or bad.

10. The belief that the world is wholly good has, nevertheless, been widely held. It has been held either because, as a part of revealed religion, the world has been supposed created by a good and omnipotent God, or because, on metaphysical grounds, it was thought possible to *prove* that the sum-total of existent things must be good. With the former line of argument we are not here concerned; the latter must be briefly dealt with.

The belief that, without assuming any ethical premiss, we can prove that the world is good, or indeed any other result containing the notion of good, logically involves the belief that the notion of good is complex and capable of definition. If when we say that a thing is good we mean (for example) that it has three other simpler properties, then, by proving that a thing has those three properties we prove that it is good, and thus we get a conclusion involving the notion of good, although our premisses did not involve it. But if good is a simple notion, no such inference will be possible; unless our premisses contain the notion of good, our conclusion cannot contain it. The case is analogous to the case of elements and compounds in chemistry. By combining elements or compounds we can get a new compound, but no chemical operation will give an element which was not present in the beginning. So, if good is simple, no propositions not containing this notion can have consequences which do contain it.

As a matter of fact, those who have endeavoured to prove

that the world as a whole is good have usually adopted the view that all evil consists wholly in the absence of something and that nothing positive is evil. This they have usually supported by defining 'good' as meaning the same as 'real'. Spinoza says:[1] 'By reality and perfection I mean the same thing'; and hence it follows, with much less trouble than metaphysicians have usually taken in the proof, that the real is perfect. This is the view in 'Abt Vogler': 'The evil is null, is nought, is silence implying sound.'

Whenever it is said that all evil is limitation, the same doctrine is involved; what is meant is that evil never consists in the existence of something which can be called bad, but only in the non-existence of something. Hence everything that does exist must be good, and the sum-total of existence, since it exists most, must be the best of all. And this view is set forth as resulting from the *meaning* of 'evil'.

The notion that non-existence is what is *meant* by 'evil' is refuted exactly as the previous definitions of 'good' were refuted. And the belief that, as a matter of fact, nothing that exists is evil, is one which no one would advocate except a metaphysician defending a theory. Pain and hatred and envy and cruelty are surely things that exist, and are not merely the absence of their opposites; but the theory should hold that they are indistinguishable from the blank unconsciousness of an oyster. Indeed, it would seem that this whole theory has been advanced solely because of the unconscious bias in favour of optimism, and that its opposite is logically just as tenable. We might urge that evil consists in existence, and good in non-existence; that therefore the sum-total of existence is the worst thing there is, and that only non-existence is good. Indeed, Buddhism does seem to maintain some such view. It is plain that this view is false; but logically it is no more absurd than its opposite.

11. We cannot, then, infer any results as to what is good or bad from a study of the things that exist. This conclusion needs chiefly, at the present time, to be applied against

[1] *Ethics,* pt. ii df. vi.

23

evolutionary ethics. The phrase 'survival of the fittest' seems to have given rise to the belief that those who survive are the fittest in some ethical sense, and that the course of evolution gives evidence that the later type is better than the earlier. On this basis, a worship of force is easily set up, and the mitigation of struggle by civilization comes to be deprecated. It is thought that what fights most successfully is most admirable, and that what does not help in fighting is worthless. Such a view is wholly destitute of logical foundation. The course of nature, as we have seen, is irrelevant in deciding as to what is good or bad. *A priori*, it would be as probable that evolution should go from bad to worse, as that it should go from good to better. What makes the view plausible is the fact that the lower animals existed earlier than the higher, and that among men the civilized races are able to defeat and often exterminate the uncivilized. But here the ethical preference of the higher to the lower animals, and of the exterminators to the exterminated, is not based upon evolution, but exists independently, and unconsciously intrudes into our judgment of the evolutionary process. If evolutionary ethics were sound, we ought to be entirely indifferent as to what the course of evolution may be, since whatever it is is thereby proved to be the best. Yet if it should turn out that the Negro or the Chinaman was able to oust the European, we should cease to have any admiration of evolution; for as a matter of fact our preference of the European to the Negro is wholly independent of the European's greater prowess with the Maxim gun.

Broadly, the fact that a thing is unavoidable affords no evidence that it is not an evil; and the fact that a thing is impossible affords no evidence that it is not a good. It is doubtless foolish, in practice, to fret over the inevitable; but it is false, in theory, to let the actual world dictate our standard of good and evil. It is evident that among the things that exist some are good, some bad, and that we know too little of the universe to have any right to an opinion as to whether the good or the bad preponderates, or as to whether either is likely in the future to gain on the other. Optimism and pessimism alike are general theories as to the universe which there is no reason whatever for accepting; what we know of the world tends to suggest that the good and the evil are fairly balanced, but it is of course possible that what we do not know is very much better or very much worse than what we do know. Complete suspense of judgment in this matter is therefore the only rational attitude.

III. RIGHT AND WRONG

12. The ideas of right and wrong conduct are, as we have seen, those with which ethics is generally supposed to be most concerned. This view, which is unduly narrow, is fostered by the use of the one word 'good', both for the sort of conduct which is *right,* and for the sort of things which ought to exist on account of their intrinsic value. This double use of the word 'good' is very confusing, and tends greatly to obscure the distinction of ends and means. I shall therefore speak of *right* actions, not of *good* actions, confining the word 'good' to the sense explained in Section II.

The word 'right' is very ambiguous, and it is by no means easy to distinguish the various meanings which it has in common parlance. Owing to the variety of these meanings, adherence to any one necessarily involves us in apparent paradoxes when we use it in a context which suggests one of the other meanings. This is the usual result of precision of language; but so long as the paradoxes are merely verbal, they do not give rise to more than verbal objections.

In judging of conduct we find at the outset two widely divergent methods, of which one is advocated by some moralists, the other by others, while both are practised by those who have no ethical theory. One of these methods, which is that advocated by utilitarians, judges the rightness of an act by relation to the goodness or badness of its consequences. The other method, advocated by intuitionists, judges by the approval or disapproval of the moral sense or conscience. I believe that it is necessary to combine both theories in order to get a complete account of right and wrong. There is, I think, one sense in which a man does right when he does what will probably have the best consequences, and another in which he does right when he follows the dictates of his conscience, whatever the probable consequences may be. (There are many other senses which we may give to the word 'right', but these two seem to be the most important.) Let us begin by considering the second of these senses.

13. The question we have to ask ourselves is: What do we mean by the dictates of the moral sense? If these are to afford a *definition* of right conduct, we cannot say that they consist in judging that such and such acts are *right*, for that would make our definition circular. We shall have to say that the moral sense consists in a certain specific *emotion* of *approval* towards an act, and that an act is to be called right when the agent, at the moment of action, feels this emotion of approval towards the action which he decides to perform. There is certainly a sense in which a man ought to perform any act which he approves, and to abstain from any act which he disapproves; and it seems also undeniable that there are emotions which may be called approval and disapproval. Thus this theory, whether adequate or not, must be allowed to contain a part of the truth.

It is, however, fairly evident that there are other meanings of right conduct, and that, though there is an emotion of approval, there is also a judgment of approval, which may or may not be true. For we certainly hold that a man who has done an action which his conscience approved may have been mistaken, and that in some sense his conscience ought not to have approved his action. But this would be impossible if nothing were involved except an emotion. To be mistaken implies a judgment; and thus we must admit that there is such a thing as a *judgment* of approval. If this were not the case we could not reason with a man as to what is right; what he approves would be necessarily right for him to do, and there could be no argument against his approval. We do in fact hold that when one man approves of a certain act, while another disapproves, one of them is mistaken, which would not be the case with a mere emotion. If one man likes oysters and another dislikes them, we do not say that either of them is mistaken.

Thus there is a judgment of approval,[1] and this must consist of a judgment that an act is, in a new sense, right. The judgment of approval is not merely the judgment that we feel the emotion of approval, for then another who disapproved would not necessarily hold our judgment of approval to be mistaken. Thus in order to give a meaning to the judgment of approval, it is necessary to admit a sense of *right* other than *approved*. In this sense, when we approve an act we judge that it is right, and we may be mistaken in so judging. This new sense is *objective*, in the sense that it does not depend upon the opinions and feelings of the agent. Thus a man who obeys the dictates of his conscience is not always acting rightly in the objective sense. When a man does what his conscience approves, he does what he *believes* to be objectively right, but not necessarily what *is* objectively right. We need, therefore, some other criterion than the moral sense for judging what is objectively right.

14. It is in defining objective rightness that the consequences of an action become relevant. Some moralists, it is true, deny the dependence upon consequences; but that is to be attributed, I think, to confusion with the subjective sense. When people argue as to whether such and such an action is right, they always adduce the consequences which it has or may be expected to have. A statesman who has to decide

[1] The judgment of approval does not always coincide with the emotion of approval. For example, when a man has been led by his reason to reject a moral code which he formerly held, it will commonly happen, at least for a time, that his emotion of approval follows the old code, though his judgment has abandoned it. Thus he may have been brought up, like Mohammed's first disciples, to believe it a duty to avenge the murder of relations by murdering the murderer or his relations; and he may continue to *feel* approval of such vengeance after he has ceased to *judge* it approvingly. The *emotion* of approval will not be again in question in what follows.

what is the right policy, or a teacher who has to decide what is the right education, will be expected to consider what policy or what education is likely to have the best results. Whenever a question is at all complicated, and cannot be settled by following some simple rule, such as 'thou shalt not steal', or 'thou shalt not bear false witness', it is at once evident that the decision cannot be made except by consideration of consequences.

But even when the decision can be made by a simple precept, such as not to lie or not to steal, the justification of the precept is found only by consideration of consequences. A code such as the Decalogue, it must be admitted, can hardly be true *without exception* if the goodness or badness of consequences is what determines the rightness or wrongness of actions; for in so complex a world it is unlikely that obedience to the Decalogue will always produce better consequences than disobedience. Yet it is a suspicious circumstance that breaches of those of the Ten Commandments which people still hold it a duty to obey do, as a matter of fact, have bad consequences in the vast majority of instances, and would not be considered wrong in a case in which it was fairly certain that their consequences would be good. This latter fact is concealed by a question-begging addition of moral overtones to words. Thus, e.g., 'thou shalt do no murder' would be an important precept if it were interpreted, as Tolstoy interprets it, to mean 'thou shalt not take human life'. But it is not so interpreted; on the contrary, some taking of human life is called 'justifiable homicide'. Thus murder comes to mean 'unjustifiable homicide'; and it is a mere tautology to say, 'Thou shalt do no unjustifiable homicide'. That this should be announced from Sinai would be as fruitless as Hamlet's report of the ghost's message: 'There's ne'er a villain, dwelling in all Denmark, but he's an arrant knave.' As a matter of fact, people do make a certain classification of homicides, and decide that certain kinds are justifiable and certain others unjustifiable. But there are many doubtful cases: tyrannicide, capital punishment, killing in war, killing in self-defence, killing in defence of others, are some of these. And if a decision is sought, it is sought usually by considering whether the consequences of actions belonging to these classes are on the whole good or bad. Thus the importance of precepts such as the Ten Commandments lies in the fact that they give simple rules, obedience to which will in almost all cases have better consequences than disobedience; and the justification of the rules is not wholly independent of consequences.

15. In common language the received code of moral rules is usually presupposed, and an action is only called *immoral* when it infringes one of these rules. Whatever does not infringe them is regarded as permissible, so that on most of the occasions of life no one course of action is marked out as alone *right*. If a man adopts a course of action which, though not contrary to the received code, will probably have bad consequences, he is called unwise rather than immoral. Now, according to the distinction we have made between objective and subjective rightness, a man may well act in a way which is objectively wrong without doing what is subjectively wrong, i.e. what his conscience disapproves. An act (roughly speaking, I shall return to this point presently) is *immoral* when a man's conscience disapproves it, but is judged only unwise or injudicious when his conscience approves it, although we judge that it will probably have bad consequences. Now the usual moral code is supposed, in common language, to be admitted by every man's conscience, so that when he infringes it, his action is not merely injudicious, but immoral; on the other hand, where the code is silent, we regard an unfortunate action as objectively but not subjectively wrong, i.e. as injudicious, but not immoral. The acceptance of a moral code has the great advantage that, in so far as its rules are objectively right, it tends to harmonize objective and subjective rightness. Thus it tends to cover all frequent cases, leaving only the rarer ones to the individual judgment of the agent. Hence when new sorts of cases become common, the moral code soon comes to deal with them; thus each profession has its own code concerning cases common

in the profession, though not outside it. But the moral code is never itself ultimate; it is based upon an estimate of probable consequences, and is essentially a method of leading men's judgment to approve what is objectively right and disapprove what is objectively wrong. And when once a fairly correct code is accepted, the exceptions to it become very much fewer than they would otherwise be, because one of the consequences of admitting exceptions is to weaken the code, and this consequence is usually bad enough to outweigh the good resulting from admitting such and such an exception. This argument, however, works in the opposite direction with a grossly incorrect code; and it is to be observed that most conventional codes embody some degree of unwarrantable selfishness, individual, professional, or national, and are thus in certain respects worthy of detestation.

16. What is objectively right, then, is in some way dependent on consequences. The most natural supposition to start from would be that the objectively right act, under any circumstances, is the one which will have the best consequences. We will define this as the *most fortunate* act. The most fortunate act, then, is the one which will produce the greatest excess of good over evil, or the least excess of evil over good (for there may be situations in which every possible act will have consequences that are on the whole bad). But we cannot maintain that the most fortunate act is always the one which is objectively right, in the sense that it is what a wise man will hold that he ought to do. For it may happen that the act which will in fact prove the most fortunate is likely, according to all the evidence at our disposal, to be less fortunate than some other. In such a case, it will be, at least in one sense, objectively wrong to go against the evidence, in spite of the actual good result of our doing so. There have certainly been some men who have done so much harm that it would have been fortunate for the world if their nurses had killed them in infancy. But if their nurses had done so their action would not have been objectively right, because the probability was that it would not have the best effects. Hence

it would seem we must take account of probability in judging of objective rightness; let us then consider whether we can say that the objectively right act is the one which will *probably* be most fortunate. I shall define this as the *wisest* act.

The *wisest* act, then, is that one which, when account is taken of all available data, gives us the greatest expectation of good on the balance, or the least expectation of evil on the balance. There is, of course, a difficulty as to what are to be considered available data; but broadly we can distinguish, in any given state of knowledge, things capable of being foreseen from things which are unpredictable. I suppose account to be taken of the general body of current knowledge, in fact the sort of consideration which people expect when they ask legal or medical advice. There is no doubt this brings us nearer to what is objectively right than we were when we were considering the actually most fortunate act. For one thing, it justifies the unavoidable limitation to not very distant consequences, which is almost always necessary if a practical decision is to be reached. For the likelihood of error in calculating distant consequences is so great that their contribution to the *probable* good or evil is very small, though their contribution to the *actual* good or evil is likely to be much greater than that of the nearer consequences. And it seems evident that what it is quite impossible to know cannot be relevant in judging as to what conduct is right. If, as is possible, a cataclysm is going to destroy life on this planet this day week, many acts otherwise useful will prove to have been wasted labour, for example, the preparation of next year's Nautical Almanac; but since we have no reason to expect such a cataclysm, the rightness or wrongness of acts is plainly to be estimated without regard to it.

17. One apparent objection at once suggests itself to the definition. Very few acts are of sufficient importance to justify such elaborate and careful consideration as is required for forming an opinion as to whether they are the wisest. Indeed, the least important decisions are often those which it would be hardest to make on purely reasonable grounds.

A man who debates on each day which of two ways of taking exercise is likely to prove most beneficial is considered absurd; the question is at once difficult and unimportant, and is therefore not worth spending time over. But although it is true that unimportant decisions ought not to be made with excessive care, there is danger of confusion if this is regarded as an objection to our definition of objective rightness. For the act which, in the case supposed, is objectively wrong is the act of deliberation, not the act decided upon as a result of deliberation. And the deliberation is condemned by our definition, for it is very unlikely that there is no more beneficial way of spending time than in debating trivial points of conduct. Thus, although the wisest act is the one which, after complete' investigation, appears likely to give the most fortunate results, yet the complete investigation required to show that it is the wisest act is only itself wise in the case of very important decisions. This is only an elaborate way of saying that a wise man will not waste time on unimportant details. Hence this apparent objection can be answered.

18. One further addition is required for the definition of the objectively right act, namely, that it must be *possible*. Among the acts whose consequences are to be considered we must not include such as are either physically impossible to perform or impossible for the agent to think of. This last condition introduces difficulties connected with determinism, which are discussed in Section IV. Ignoring these difficulties, we may say that the objectively right act is that one which, of all that are possible, will probably have the best consequences.

19. We must now return to the consideration of subjective rightness, with a view to distinguishing conduct which is merely mistaken from conduct which is immoral or blameworthy. We here require a new sense of *ought*, which it is by no means easy to define. In the objective sense, a man ought to do what is objectively right. But in the subjective sense, which we have now to examine, he sometimes ought to do what is objectively wrong. For example, we saw that it is often

objectively right to give less consideration to an unimportant question of conduct than would be required for forming a trustworthy judgment as to what is objectively right. Now it seems plain that if we have given to such a question the amount and kind of consideration which is objectively right, and we then do what *appears* to us objectively right, our action is, in some sense, subjectively right, although it may be objectively wrong. Our action could certainly not be called a sin, and might even be highly virtuous, in spite of its objective wrongness. It is these notions of what is sinful and what is virtuous that we have now to consider.

20. The first suggestion that naturally occurs is that an act is subjectively right when it is judged by the agent to be objectively right, and subjectively wrong when it is judged to be objectively wrong. I do not mean that it is subjectively right when the agent judges that it is the act which, of all that are possible, will probably have the best results; for the agent may not accept the above account of objective rightness. I mean merely that it is the one towards which he has the judgment of approval. A man may judge an act to be right without judging that its consequences will be probably the best possible; I only contend that, when he *truly* judges it to be right, then its consequences will probably be the best possible. But his judgment as to what is objectively right may err, not only by a wrong estimate of probable consequences, or by failing to think of an act which he might have thought of, but also by a wrong theory as to what constitutes objective rightness. In other words, the definition I gave of objective rightness is not meant as an analysis of the meaning of the word, but as a mark which in fact attaches to all objectively right actions and to no others.

We are to consider then the suggestion that an act is moral when the agent approves it and immoral when he disapproves it; using 'moral' to mean 'subjectively right' and 'immoral' to mean 'subjectively wrong'. This suggestion, it is plain, will not stand without much modification. In the first place, we often hold it immoral to approve some things and disapprove others, unless there are special circumstances to excuse such approval or disapproval. In the second place, unreflecting acts, in which there is no judgment either of approval or disapproval, are often moral or immoral. For both these reasons the suggested definition must be regarded as inadequate.

21. The doctrine that an act is never immoral when the agent thinks it right has the drawback (or the advantage) that it excuses almost all the acts which would be commonly condemned. Very few people deliberately do what, at the moment, they believe to be wrong; usually they first argue themselves into a belief that what they wish to do is right. They decide that it is their duty to teach so-and-so a lesson, that their rights have been so grossly infringed that if they take no revenge there will be an encouragement to injustice, that without a moderate indulgence in pleasure a character cannot develop in the best way, and so on and so on. Yet we do not cease to blame them on that account. Of course it may be said that a belief produced by a course of self-deception is not a genuine belief, and that the people who invent such excuses for themselves know all the while that the truth is the other way. Up to a point this is no doubt true, though I doubt if it is always true. There are, however, other cases of mistaken judgment as to what is right, where the judgment is certainly genuine, and yet we blame the agent. These are cases of thoughtlessness, where a man remembers consequences to himself, but forgets consequences to others. In such a case he may judge correctly and honestly on all the data that he remembers, yet if he were a better man he would remember more data. Most of the actions commonly condemned as selfish probably come under this head. Hence we must admit that an act may be immoral, even if the agent quite genuinely judges that it is right.

Unreflecting acts, again, in which there is no judgment as to right or wrong, are often praised or blamed. Acts of generosity, for example, are more admired when they are impulsive than when they result from reflection. I cannot think of any act which is more blamed when it is impulsive than when it is deliberate; but certainly many impulsive acts are blamed—for example, such as spring from an impulse of malice or cruelty.

22. In all these cases where reflection is absent, and also in the case of inadequate reflection, it may be said that blame does not belong properly to the act, but rather to the character revealed by the act, or, if to some acts, then to those previous deliberate acts by which the character has been produced which has resulted in the present act. The cases of self-deception would then be dismissed on the ground that the self-deceiver never really believes what he wishes to believe. We could then retain our original definition, that a moral act is one which the agent judges to be right, while an immoral one is one which he judges to be wrong. But I do not think this would accord with what most people really mean. I rather think that a moral act should be defined as one which the agent would have judged to be right if he had considered the question candidly and with due care; if, that is to say, he had examined the data before him with a view to discovering what was right, and not with a view to proving such and such a course to be right. If an act is unimportant, and at the same time not obviously less right than some obvious alternative, we shall consider it neither moral nor immoral; for in such a case the act does not deserve careful consideration. The amount of care which a decision deserves depends upon its importance and difficulty; in the case of a statesman advocating a new policy, for example, years of deliberation may sometimes be necessary to excuse him from the charge of levity. But with less important acts, it is usually right to decide even when further reflection might show the present decision to be erroneous. Thus there is a certain amount of reflection appropriate to various acts, while some right acts are best when they spring from impulse (though these are such as reflection would approve). We may therefore say that an act is moral when it is one which the agent would judge to be right after an appropriate amount of candid thought, or, in the case of acts which are best when they are un-

reflecting, after the amount and kind of thought requisite to form a first opinion. An act is immoral when the agent would judge it to be wrong after an appropriate amount of reflection. It is neither moral nor immoral when it is unimportant and a small amount of reflection would not suffice to show whether it was right or wrong.

23. We may now sum up our discussion of right and wrong. When a man asks himself: 'What ought I to do?' he is asking what conduct is *right* in an objective sense. He cannot mean: 'What ought a person to do who holds my views as to what a person ought to do?' for his views as to what a person ought to do are what will constitute his answer to the question 'What ought I to do?' But the onlooker, who thinks that the man has answered this question wrongly, may nevertheless hold that, in acting upon his answer, the man was acting rightly in a second, subjective, sense. This second sort of right action we call *moral* action. We held that an action is *moral* when the agent would judge it to be *right* after an appropriate amount of candid thought, or after a small amount in the case of acts which are best when they are unreflecting; the appropriate amount of thought being dependent upon the difficulty and the importance of the decision. And we held that an action is *right* when, of all that are possible, it is the one which will probably have the best results. There are many other meanings of *right*, but these seem to be the meanings required for answering the questions: 'What ought I to do?' and 'What acts are immoral?'

IV. DETERMINISM AND MORALS

24. The importance to ethics of the free-will question is a subject upon which there has existed almost as much diversity of opinion as on the free-will question itself. It has been urged by advocates of free-will that its denial involves the denial of merit and demerit, and that, with the denial of these, ethics collapses. It has been urged on the other side that, unless we can foresee, at least partially, the consequences of our actions,

it is impossible to know what course we ought to take under any given circumstances; and that if other people's actions cannot be in any degree predicted, the foresight required for rational action becomes impossible. I do not propose, in the following discussion, to go into the free-will controversy itself. The grounds in favour of determinism appear to me overwhelming, and I shall content myself with a brief indication of these grounds. The question I am concerned with is not the freewill question itself, but the question how, if at all, morals are affected by assuming determinism.

In considering this question, as in most of the other problems of ethics, the moralist who has not had a philosophical training appears to me to go astray, and become involved in needless complications, through supposing that right and wrong in conduct are the ultimate conceptions of ethics, rather than good and bad, in the *effects* of conduct and in other things. The words 'good' and 'bad' are used both for the sort of conduct which is *right* or *wrong,* and for the sort of effects to be expected from right and wrong conduct, respectively. We speak of a *good* picture, a *good* dinner, and so on, as well as of a *good* action. But there is a great difference between these two meanings of *good.* Roughly speaking, a *good* action is one of which the probable effects are *good* in the other sense. It is confusing to have two meanings for one word, and we therefore agreed in the previous section to speak of a *right* action rather than a *good* action. In order to decide whether an action is *right,* it is necessary, as we have seen, to consider its probable effects. If the probable effects are, on the whole, better than those of any other action which is possible under the circumstances, then the action is *right.* The things that are good are things which, on their own account, and apart from any consideration of their effects, we ought to wish to see in existence: they are such things as, we may suppose, might make the world appear to the Creator worth creating. I do not wish to deny that right conduct is among the things that are good on their own account; but if it is so, it depends for its intrinsic goodness upon the goodness of those other things which it aims at producing, such as love or happiness. Thus the rightness of conduct is not the fundamental conception upon which ethics is built up. This fundamental conception is intrinsic goodness or badness.

As the outcome of our discussions in the previous section, I shall assume the following definitions. The *objectively right* action, in any circumstances, is that action which, of all that are possible, gives us, when account is taken of all available data, the greatest expectation of probable good effects, or the least expectation of probable bad effects. The *subjectively right* or *moral* action is that one which will be judged by the agent to be objectively right if he devotes to the question an appropriate amount of candid thought, or, in the case of actions that ought to be impulsive, a small amount. The appropriate amount of thought depends upon the importance of the action and the difficulty of the decision. An act is neither moral nor immoral when it is unimportant, and a small amount of reflection would not suffice to show whether it was right or wrong. After these preliminaries, we can pass to the consideration of our main topic.

25. The principle of causality—that every event is determined by previous events, and can (theoretically) be predicted when enough previous events are known—appears to apply just as much to human actions as to other events. It cannot be said that its application to human actions, or to any other phenomena, is wholly beyond doubt; but a doubt extending to the principle of causality must be so fundamental as to involve all science, all everyday knowledge, and everything, or almost everything, that we believe about the actual world. If causality is doubted, morals collapse, since a right action, as we have seen, is one of which the probable effects are the best possible, so that estimates of right and wrong necessarily presuppose that our actions can have effects, and therefore that the law of causality holds. In favour of the view that human actions alone are not the effects of causes, there appears to be no ground whatever except the sense of spontaneity. But the sense of spontaneity only affirms that

we can do as we choose, and choose as we please, which no determinist denies; it cannot affirm that our choice is independent of all motives,[1] and indeed introspection tends rather to show the opposite. It is said by the advocates of free-will[2] that determinism destroys morals, since it shows that all our actions are inevitable, and that therefore they deserve neither praise nor blame. Let us consider how far, if at all, this is the case.

26. The part of ethics which is concerned, not with conduct, but with the meaning of good and bad, and the things that are intrinsically good and bad, is plainly quite independent of freewill. Causality belongs to the description of the existing world, and we saw that no inference can be drawn from what exists to what is good. Whether, then, causality holds always, sometimes, or never is a question wholly irrelevant in the consideration of intrinsic goods and evils. But .when we come to conduct and the notion of *ought*, we cannot be sure that determinism makes no difference. For we saw that the objectively right action may be defined as that one which, of all that are *possible* under the circumstances, will probably on the whole have the best consequences. The action which is objectively right must therefore be in some sense *possible*. But if determinism is true, there is a sense in which no action is possible except the one actually performed. Hence, if the two senses of possibility are the same, the action actually performed is always objectively right; for it is the only possible action, and therefore there is no other possible action which would have had better results. There is here, I think, a real difficulty. But let us consider the various kinds of possibility which may be meant.

In order that an act may be a *possible* act, it must be physically possible to perform, it must be possible to think of, and it must be possible to choose if we think of it. Physical

---

[1] A *motive* means merely a *cause of volition*.

[2] I use *freewill* to mean the doctrine that not all volitions are determined by causes, which is the denial of determinism. Freewill is often used in senses compatible with determinism, but I am not concerned to affirm or deny it in such senses.

possibility, to begin with, is obviously necessary. There are circumstances under which I might do a great deal of good by running from Oxford to London in five minutes. But I should not be called unwise, or guilty of an objectively wrong act, for omitting to do so. We may define an act as physically possible when it will occur if I will it. Acts for which this condition fails are not to be taken account of in estimating rightness or wrongness.

27. To judge whether an act is possible to think of is more difficult, but we certainly take account of it in judging what a man ought to do. There is no *physical* impossibility about employing one's spare moments in writing lyric poems better than any yet written, and this would certainly be a more useful employment than most people find for their spare moments. But we do not blame people for not writing lyric poems unless, like FitzGerald, they are people that we feel could have written them. And not only do we not blame them, but we feel that their action may be objectively as well as subjectively right if it is the wisest that *they* could have thought of. But what they *could* have thought of is not the same as what they *did* think of. Suppose a man in a fire or a shipwreck becomes so panic-stricken that he never for a moment thinks of the help that is due to other people, we do not on that account hold that he does right in only thinking of himself. Hence in some sense (though it is not quite clear what this sense is), some of the courses of action which a man does not think of are regarded as possible for him to think of, though others are admittedly impossible.

There is thus a sense in which it must be possible to think of an action, if we are to hold that it is objectively wrong not to perform the action. There is also, if determinism is true, a sense in which it is not possible to think of any action except those which we do think of. But it is questionable whether these two senses of possibility are the same. A man who finds that his house is on fire may run out of it in a panic without thinking of warning the other inmates; but we *feel*, rightly or wrongly, that it was possible for him to think of warning them in a sense in which it is not possible for a prosaic person to think of a lyric poem. It may be that we are wrong in feeling this difference, and that what really distinguishes the two cases is dependence upon past decisions. That is to say, we may recognize that no different choice among alternatives thought of at any time would have turned an ordinary man into a good lyric poet; but that most men, by suitably choosing among alternatives actually thought of, can acquire the sort of character which will lead them to remember their neighbours in a fire. And if a man engages in some useful occupation of which a natural effect is to destroy his nerve, we may conceivably hold that this excuses his panic in an emergency. In such a point, it would seem that our judgment may really be dependent on the view we take as to the existence of freewill; for the believer in freewill cannot allow any such excuse.

If we try to state the difference we feel between the case of the lyric poems and the case of the fire, it seems to come to this: that we do not hold an act objectively wrong when it would have required what we recognize as a special aptitude in order to think of a better act, and when we believe that the agent did not possess this aptitude. But this distinction seems to imply that there is not such a thing as a special aptitude for this or that virtue; a view which cannot, I think, be maintained. An aptitude for generosity or for kindness may be as much a natural gift as an aptitude for poetry; and an aptitude for poetry may be as much improved by practice as an aptitude for kindness or generosity. Thus it would seem that there is no sense in which it is possible to think of some actions which in fact we do not think of, but impossible to think of others, except the sense that the ones we regard as possible would have been thought of if a different choice among alternatives actually thought of had been made on some previous occasion. We shall then modify our previous definition of the objectively right action by saying that it is the probably most beneficial among those that occur to the agent at the moment of choice. But we shall hold that, in certain cases, the fact that a more beneficial alternative does not occur to him is evidence of a wrong choice on some previous occasion.

28. But since occasions of choice do often arise, and since there certainly is a sense in which it is possible to choose any one of a number of different actions which we think of, we can still distinguish some actions as right and some as wrong. Our previous definitions of objectively right actions and of moral actions still hold, with the modification that, among physically possible actions, only those *which we actually think of* are to be regarded as possible. When several alternative actions present themselves, it is certain that we can both do which we choose, and choose which we will. In this sense all the alternatives are possible. What determinism maintains is, that our will to choose this or that alternative is the effect of antecedents; but this does not prevent our will from being itself a cause of other effects. And the sense in which different decisions are possible seems sufficient to distinguish some actions as right and some as wrong, some as moral and some as immoral.

Connected with this is another sense in which, when we deliberate, either decision is possible. The fact that we judge one course objectively right may be the cause of our choosing this course: thus, before we have decided as to which course we think right, either is possible in the sense that either will result from our decision as to which we think right. This sense of possibility is important to the moralist, and illustrates the fact that determinism does not make moral deliberation futile.

29. Determinism does not, therefore, destroy the distinction of right and wrong; and we saw before that it does not destroy the distinction of good and bad: we shall still be able to regard some people as better than others, and some actions as more right than others. But it is said that praise and blame and responsibility are destroyed by determinism. When a madman commits what in a sane man we should call a crime, we do not blame him, partly because he probably cannot

judge rightly as to consequences, but partly also because we feel that he could not have done otherwise: if all men are really in the position of the madman, it would seem that all ought to escape blame. But I think the question of choice really decides as to praise and blame. The madman, we believe (excluding the case of wrong judgment as to consequences), did not choose between different courses, but was impelled by a blind impulse. The sane man who (say) commits a murder has, on the contrary, either at the time of the murder or at some earlier time, chosen the worst of two or more alternatives that occurred to him; and it is for this we blame him. It is true that the two cases merge into each other, and the madman may be blamed if he has become mad in consequence of vicious self-indulgence. But it is right that the two cases should not be too sharply distinguished, for we know how hard it often is in practice to decide whether people are what is called 'responsible for their actions'. It is sufficient that there is a distinction, and that it can be applied easily in most cases, though there are marginal cases which present difficulties. We apply praise or blame, then, and we attribute responsibility, where a man, having to exercise choice, has chosen wrongly; and this sense of praise or blame is not destroyed by determinism.

30. Determinism, then, does not in any way interfere with morals. It is worth noticing that freewill, on the contrary, would interfere most seriously, if anybody really believed in it. People never do, as a matter of fact, believe that anyone else's actions are not determined by motives, however much they may think *themselves* free. Bradshaw consists entirely of predictions as to the actions of engine-drivers; but no one doubts Bradshaw on the ground that the volitions of engine-drivers are not governed by motives. If we really believed that other people's actions did not have causes, we could never try to influence other people's actions; for such influence can only result if we know, more or less, what causes will produce the actions we desire. If we could never try to influence other people's actions, no man could try to get

elected to Parliament, or ask a woman to marry him: argument, exhortation, and command would become mere idle breath. Thus almost all the actions with which morality is concerned would become irrational, rational action would be wholly precluded from trying to influence people's volitions, and right and wrong would be interfered with in a way in which determinism certainly does not interfere with them. Most morality absolutely depends upon the assumption that volitions have causes, and nothing in morals is destroyed by this assumption.

Most people, it is true, do not hold the freewill doctrine in so extreme a form as that against which we have been arguing. They would hold that most of a man's actions have causes, but that some few, say one per cent, are uncaused spontaneous assertions of will. If this view is taken, unless we can mark off the one per cent of volitions which are uncaused, every inference as to human actions is infected with what we may call one per cent of doubt. This, it must be admitted, would not matter much in practice, because, on other grounds, there will usually be at least one per cent of doubt in predictions as to human actions. But from the standpoint of theory there is a wide difference: the sort of doubt that must be admitted in any case is a sort which is capable of indefinite diminution, while the sort derived from the possible intervention of freewill is absolute and ultimate. In so far, therefore, as the possibility of uncaused volitions comes in, all the consequences above pointed out follow; and in so far as it does not come in, determinism holds. Thus one per cent of freewill has one per cent of the objectionableness of absolute freewill, and has also only one per cent of the ethical consequences.

In fact, however, no one really holds that right acts are uncaused. It would be a monstrous paradox to say that a man's decision ought not to be influenced by his belief as to what is his duty; yet, if he allows himself to decide on an act because he believes it to be his duty, his decision has a motive, i.e. a cause, and is not free in the only sense in which the determinist must deny freedom. It would seem, therefore, that the objections to determinism are mainly attributable to misunderstanding of its purport. Hence, finally it is not determinism but freewill that has subversive consequences. There is therefore no reason to regret that the grounds in favour of determinism are overwhelmingly strong.

V. EGOISM

31. We have next to consider an objection to the view that objective rightness consists in probably having the best consequences on the whole. The objection I mean is that of egoism: that a man's first duty is to himself, and that to secure his own good is more imperative than to secure other people's. Extensions of this view are, that a man should prefer the interest of his family to that of strangers, of his countrymen to that of foreigners, or of his friends to that of his enemies. All these views have in common the belief that, quite apart from practicability, the ends which one man ought to pursue are different from those which another man ought to pursue.

Egoism has several different meanings. It may mean that every man is psychologically bound to pursue his own good exclusively; it may mean that every man will achieve the best result on the whole by pursuing his own good; it may mean that his own good is the only thing a man ought to think good; and it may mean, lastly, that there is no such thing as the general good at all, but only individual goods, and that each man is only concerned with what is good for himself. These meanings all presuppose that we know what is meant by '*my* good'; but this is not an easy conception to define clearly. I shall therefore begin by considering what it is capable of meaning.

32. 'My good' is a phrase capable of many different meanings. It may mean any good that I desire, whether this has any further special relation to me or not. Or, again, it may mean my pleasure, or any state of mind in me which is good. Or it may include honour and respect from others, or

anything which is a good and has some relation to me in virtue of which it can be considered *mine*. The two meanings with which we shall be concerned are: (1) any good I desire, (2) any good having to me some relation other than that I desire it, which it does not have to others, of the kind which makes it *mine*, as my pleasure, my reputation, my learning, my virtue, etc.

The theory that every man is psychologically bound to pursue his own good exclusively is, I think, inconsistent with known facts of human nature, unless 'my good' is taken in the sense of 'something which I desire', and even then I do not necessarily pursue what I desire most strongly. The important point is, that what I desire has not necessarily any such other relation to me as would make it my good in the second of the above senses. This is the point which must now occupy us.

If 'my good' means a good which is mine in some other sense than that I desire it, then I think it can be shown that my good is by no means the only object of my actions. There is a common confusion in people's thoughts on this subject, namely the following: If I desire anything, its attainment will give me more or less pleasure, and its non-attainment will give me more or less pain. Hence it is inferred that I desire it on account of the pleasure it would give me, and not on its own account. But this is to put the cart before the horse. The pleasure we get from things usually depends upon our having had a desire which they satisfy; the pleasures of eating and drinking, for example, depend upon hunger and thirst. Or take, again, the pleasure people get from the victory of their own party in a contest. Other people would derive just the same pleasure from the victory of the opposite party; in each case the pleasure depends for its existence upon the desire, and would not exist if the desire had not existed. Thus we cannot say that people only desire pleasure. They desire all kinds of things, and pleasures come from desires much oftener than desires from imagined pleasures. Thus the mere fact that a man will derive some pleasure from achieving his object is no reason for saying that his desire is self-centred.

33. Such arguments are necessary for the refutation of those who hold it to be obvious *a priori* that every man must always pursue his own good exclusively. But, as is often the case with refutations of *a priori* theories, there is an air of logic-chopping about a discussion as to whether desire or the pleasure expected from its satisfaction ought to have priority. Let us leave these questions, and consider whether, as a matter of fact, people's actions can be explained on the egoistic hypothesis. The most obvious instances to the contrary are, of course, cases of self-sacrifice—of men to their country, for example, or of parents to children. But these instances are so obvious that the egoistic theory is ready with an answer. It will maintain that, in such cases, the people who make the sacrifice would not be happy if they did not make it, that they desire the applause of men or of their own consciences, that they find in the moment of sacrifice an exaltation which realizes their highest self, etc., etc., etc. Let us examine these arguments. It is said that the people in question would not be happy if they did not make the sacrifice. This is often false in fact, but we may let that pass. Why would they not be happy? Either because others would think less well of them, or because they themselves would feel pangs of conscience, or because they genuinely desired the object to be attained by their sacrifice and could not be happy without it. In the last case they have admittedly a desire not centred in self; the supposed effect upon their happiness is due to the desire, and would not otherwise exist, so that the effect upon happiness cannot be brought into account for the desire. But if people may have desires for things that lie outside their ego, then such desires, like others, may determine action, and it is possible to pursue an object which is not 'my' good in any sense except that I desire and pursue it. Thus, in all cases of self-sacrifice, those who hold the egoistic theory will have to maintain that the outside end secured by the self-sacrifice is not desired. When a soldier sacrifices his life he does not desire the victory of his country, and so on. This is already sufficiently preposterous, and sufficiently contrary to plain

fact. But it is not enough. Assuming that this is the case, let us suppose that self-sacrifice is dictated, not by desire for any outside end, but by fear of the disapproval of others. If this were so there would be no self-sacrifice if no one would know of its non-performance. A man who saw another drowning would not try to save him if he was sure that no one would see him not jumping into the water. This also is plainly contrary to fact. It may be said that the desire for approval, as well as the fear of disapproval, ought to be taken into account; and a man can always make sure of approval by judicious boasting. But men have made sacrifices universally disapproved, for example, in maintaining unpopular opinions; and very many have made sacrifices of which an essential part was that they should not be mentioned. Hence the defender of psychological egoism is driven back on the approval of conscience as the motive to an act of self-sacrifice. But it is really impossible to believe that all who deny themselves are so destitute of rational foresight as this theory implies. The pangs of conscience are to most people a very endurable pain, and practice in wrong-doing rapidly diminishes them. And if the act of self-denial involves the loss of life, the rapture of self-approbation, which the virtuous man is supposed to be seeking, must in any case be very brief. I conclude that the psychology of egoism is only produced by the exigencies of a wrong theory, and is not in accordance with the facts of observable human nature.

Thus when we consider human actions and desires apart from preconceived theories, it is obvious that most of them are objective and have no direct reference to self. If 'my good' means an object belonging to me in the sense of being a state of my mind, or a whole of which a state of my mind is a part, or what others think about me, then it is false that I can only desire or pursue my good. The only sense in which it is true is when 'my good' is taken to mean 'what I desire'; but what I desire need not have any other connection with myself, except that I desire it. Thus there is no truth in the doctrine that men do, as a matter of fact, only desire or pursue objects specially related to themselves in any way except as objects desired or pursued.

34. The next form of egoism to be considered is the doctrine that every man will best serve the general good by pursuing his own. There is a comfortable eighteenth-century flavour about this doctrine—it suggests a good income, a good digestion, and an enviable limitation of sympathy. We may admit at once that in a well-ordered world it would be true, and even that, as society becomes better organized, it becomes progressively truer, since rewards will more and more be attached to useful actions. And in so far as a man's own good is more in his control than other people's, his actions will rightly concern themselves more with it than with other people's. For the same reason he will be more concerned with the good of his family than with that of people with whom he has less to do, and more with the good of his own country than with that of foreign countries. But the scope of such considerations is strictly limited, and everyone can easily find in his own experience cases where the general good has been served by what at any rate appears to be a self-sacrifice. If such cases are to be explained away, it is necessary to alter the conception of 'my own good' in a way which destroys the significance of the doctrine we are considering. It may be said, for example, that the greatest of goods is a virtuous life. It will then follow that whoever lives a virtuous life secures for himself the greatest of goods. But if the doctrine means to assert, as it usually does, that self-centred desires, if they are prudent and enlightened, will suffice to produce the most useful conduct, then a refutation may be obtained either from common experience or from any shining example of public merit. The reformer is almost always a man who has strong desires for objects quite unconnected with himself; and indeed this is a characteristic of all who are not petty-minded. I think the doctrine depends for its plausibility, like psychological egoism, upon regarding every object which I desire as *my* good, and supposing that it must be mine in some other sense than that I desire it.

49

35. The doctrine that my good is the only thing that I ought to think good can only be logically maintained by those who hold that I ought to believe what is false. For if I am right in thinking that my good is the only good, then everyone else is mistaken unless he admits that my good, not his, is the only good. But this is an admission which I can scarcely hope that others will be willing to make.

But what is really intended is, as a rule, to deny that there is any such thing as the general good at all. This doctrine cannot be logically refuted, unless by discovering in those who maintain it some opinion which implies the opposite. If a man were to maintain that there is no such thing as colour, for example, we should be unable to disprove his position, provided he was careful to think out its implications. As a matter of fact, however, everybody does hold opinions which imply a general good. Everybody judges that some sorts of communities are better than others; and most people who affirm that when they say a thing is good they mean merely that they desire it, would admit that it is better two people's desires should be satisfied than only one person's. In some such way people fail to carry out the doctrine that there is no such concept as *good*; and if there is such a concept, then what is good is not good *for me* or *for you*, but is simply good. The denial that there is such a thing as good in an impersonal sense is only possible, therefore, to those who are content to have no ethics at all.

36. It is possible to hold that, although there is such a thing as the general good, and although this is not always best served by pursuing my own good, yet it is always right to pursue my own good exclusively. This doctrine is not now often held as regards individuals; but in international politics it is commonly held as regards nations. Many Englishmen and many Germans would admit that it is right for an English statesman to pursue exclusively the good of England, and a German the good of Germany, even if that good is to be attained by greater injury to the other. It is difficult to see what grounds there can be for such a view. If good is to be

pursued at all, it can hardly be relevant who is going to enjoy the good. It would be as reasonable for a man on Sundays to think only of his welfare on future Sundays, and on Mondays to think only of Mondays. The doctrine, in fact, seems to have no merit except that it justifies acts otherwise unjustifiable. It is, indeed, so evident that it is better to secure a greater good for A than a lesser good for B, that it is hard to find any still more evident principle by which to prove this. And if A happens to be someone else, and B to be myself, that cannot affect the question, since it is irrelevant to the general maxim who A and B may be.

If no form of egoism is valid, it follows that an act which ought to be performed may involve a self-sacrifice not compensated by any personal good acquired by means of such an act. So unwilling, however, are people to admit self-sacrifice as an ultimate duty that they will often defend theological dogmas on the ground that such dogmas reconcile self-interest with duty. Such reconciliations, it should be observed, are in any case merely external; they do not show that duty *means* the pursuit of one's own interest, but only that the acts which it dictates are those that further one's own interest. Thus when it is pretended that there are *logical* grounds making such reconciliations imperative, we must reply that the *logical* purpose aimed at could only be secured by showing that duty *means* the same as self-interest. It is sometimes said that the two maxims, 'You ought to aim at producing the greatest possible good' and 'You ought to pursue your own interest', are equally evident; and each is supposed to be true in all possible circumstances and in all possible worlds. But if that were the case, a world where self-interest and the general good might conflict ought not only to be non-existent, but inconceivable; yet so far is it from being inconceivable that many people conceive it to be exemplified in the actual world. Hence the view that honesty is the best policy may be a comfort to the reluctant saint, but cannot be a solution to the perplexed logician. The notion, therefore, that a good God or a future life can be *logically* inferred to remove the apparent conflict of self-interest and the general good is quite unwarrantable. If there were a logical puzzle, it could only be removed by showing that self-interest and the general good *mean* the same thing, not by showing that they coincide in fact. But if the above discussion has been sound, there is no logical puzzle: we ought to pursue the general good, and when this conflicts with self-interest, self-interest ought to give way.

VI. METHODS OF ESTIMATING GOODS AND EVILS

37. In order to complete our account of ethics, it would be natural to give a list of the principal goods and evils of which we have experience. I shall, however, not attempt to give such a list, since I hold that the reader is probably quite as capable as I am of judging what things are good and what bad. All that I propose to do in this section is to examine the view that we can never know what is good and what bad, and to suggest methods to be employed and fallacies to be avoided in considering intrinsic goodness or badness.

There is a widespread ethical scepticism, which is based upon observation of men's differences in regard to ethical questions. It is said that A thinks one thing good, and B thinks another, and there is no possible way in which either can persuade the other that he is wrong. Hence, it is concluded, the whole thing is really only a matter of taste, and it is a waste of time to ask which is right when two people differ in a judgment of value.

It would be absurd to deny that, as compared with physical science, ethics does suffer from a measure of the defect which such sceptics allege. It must be admitted that ultimately the judgment 'this thing is good' or 'that thing is bad' must be an immediate judgment, which results merely from considering the thing appraised, and cannot be proved by any argument that would appeal to a man who had passed an opposite immediate judgment. I think it must also be admitted that, even after every possible precaution against error has been taken, people's immediate judgments of value do still differ more or less. But such immediate differences seem to me to be the exception: most of the actual differences are of a kind which argument might lessen, since usually the opinion held is either one of which the opposite is demonstrable or one which is falsely believed to be itself demonstrable. This second alternative embraces all false beliefs held because they flow from a false theory; and such beliefs, though often the direct contraries of what immediate inspection would lead to, are apt to be a complete bar to inspection. This is a very familiar phenomenon. Sydney Smith, believed to be always witty, says 'pass the mustard', and the whole table is convulsed with laughter. Much wrong judgment in ethics is of this nature.

38. In regard to the things that are good or bad, in themselves, and not merely on account of their effects, there are two opposite errors of this sort to be avoided—the one the error of the philosopher, the other that of the moralist. The philosopher, bent on the construction of a system, is inclined to symplify the facts unduly, to give them a symmetry which is fictitious, and to twist them into a form in which they can all be deduced from one or two general principles. The moralist, on the other hand, being primarily concerned with conduct, tends to become absorbed in means, to value the actions men ought to perform more than the ends which such actions serve. This latter error—for in theorizing it is an error—is so forced upon us by the exigencies of practice that we may easily come to feel the ultimate ends of life far less important than the proximate and intermediate purposes which we consciously endeavour to realize. And hence most of what they value in this world would have to be omitted by many moralists from any imagined heaven, because there such things as self-denial and effort and courage and pity could find no place. The philosopher's error is less common than the moralist's, because the love of system and of the intellectual satisfaction of a deductive edifice is rarer than the love of virtue. But among writers on ethics the philo-

sopher's error occurs oftener than the other, because such writers are almost always among the few men who have the love of system. Kant has the bad eminence of combining both errors in the highest possible degree, since he holds that there is nothing good except the virtuous will—a view which simplifies the good as much as any philosopher could wish, and mistakes means for ends as completely as any moralist could enjoin.

39. The moralist's fallacy illustrates another important point. The immediate judgments which are required in ethics concern intrinsic goods and evils, not right and wrong conduct. I do not wish to deny that people have immediate judgments of right and wrong, nor yet that in action it is usually moral to follow such judgments. What I mean is that such judgments are not among those which ethics must accept without proof, provided that (whether by the suggestions of such judgments or otherwise) we have accepted some such general connection of right action with good consequences as was advocated in Section III. For then, if we know what is good and bad, we can discover what is right or wrong; hence in regard to right and wrong it is unnecessary to rely upon immediate inspection—a method which must be allowed some scope, but should be allowed as little as possible.

I think when attention is clearly confined to good and bad, as opposed to right and wrong, the amount of disagreement between different people is seen to be much less than might at first be thought. Right and wrong, since they depend upon consequences, will vary as men's circumstances vary, and will be largely affected, in particular, by men's beliefs about right and wrong, since many acts will in all likelihood have a worse effect if they are generally believed to be wrong than if they are generally believed to be right, while with some acts the opposite is the case. (For example, a man who, in exceptional circumstances, acts contrary to a received and generally true moral rule, is more likely to be right if he will be thought to be wrong, for then his action will have less tendency to weaken the authority of the rule.) Thus differences as regards rules of right action are not a ground for scepticism, provided the different rules are held in different societies. Yet such differences are in practice a very powerful solvent of ethical beliefs.

40. Some differences as to what is good in itself must, however, be acknowledged even when all possible care has been taken to consider the question by itself. For example, retributive punishment, as opposed to deterrent or reformative punishment, was almost universally considered good until a recent time; yet in our own day it is very generally condemned. Hell can only be justified if retributive punishment is good; and the decay of a belief in hell appears to be mainly due to a change of feeling on this point.

But even where there seems to be a difference as to ends, this difference is often due to some theory on one side or on both, and not to immediate inspection. Thus in the case of hell, people may reason, consciously or unconsciously, that revelation shows that God created hell, and that therefore retributive punishment must be good; and this argument doubtless influences many who would otherwise hold retributive punishment to be bad. Where there is such an influence we do not have a genuine difference in an immediate judgment as to intrinsic good or bad; and in fact such differences are, I believe, very rare indeed.

41. A source of apparent differences is that some things which in isolation are bad or indifferent are essential ingredients in what is good as a whole, and some things which are good or indifferent are essential ingredients in what is bad as a whole. In such cases we judge differently according as we are considering a thing in isolation or as an ingredient in some larger whole. To judge whether a thing is in itself good, we have to ask ourselves whether we should value it if it existed otherwise than as an ingredient in some whole which we value. But to judge whether a thing ought to exist, we have to consider whether it is a part of some whole which we value so much that we prefer the existence of the whole

with its possibly bad part to the existence of neither. Thus compassion is a good of which someone's misfortune is an essential part; envy is an evil of which someone's good is an essential part. Hence the position of some optimists, that all the evil in the world is necessary to constitute the best possible whole, is not logically absurd, though there is, so far as I know, no evidence in its favour. Similarly the view that all the good is an unavoidable ingredient in the worst possible whole is not logically absurd; but this view, not being agreeable, has found no advocates.

Even where none of the parts of a good whole are bad, or of a bad whole good, it often happens that the value of a complex whole cannot be measured by adding together the values of its parts; the whole is often better or worse than the sum of the values of its parts. In all aesthetic pleasures, for example, it is important that the object admired should really be beautiful: in the admiration of what is ugly there is something ridiculous, or even sometimes repulsive, although, apart from the object, there may be no difference in the value of the emotion *per se*. And yet, apart from the admiration it may produce, a beautiful object, if it is inanimate, appears to be neither good nor bad. Thus in themselves an ugly object and the emotion it excites in a person of bad taste may be respectively just as good as a beautiful object and the emotion it excites in a person of good taste; yet we consider the enjoyment of what is beautiful to be better, as a whole, than an exactly similar enjoyment of what is ugly. If we did not we should be foolish not to encourage bad taste, since ugly objects are much easier to produce than beautiful ones. In like manner, we consider it better to love a good person than a bad one. Titania's love for Bottom may be as lyric as Juliet's for Romeo; yet Titania is laughed at. Thus many goods must be estimated as wholes, not piecemeal; and exactly the same applies to evils. In such cases the wholes may be called *organic unities*.

42. Many theorists who have some simple account of the sole good have also, probably without having recognized

them as such, immediate judgments of value inconsistent with their theory, from which it appears that their theory is not really derived from immediate judgments of value. Thus those who have held that virtue is the sole good have generally also held that in heaven it will be *rewarded* by happiness. Yet a reward must be a good; thus they plainly *feel* that happiness also is a good. If virtue were the sole good it would be logically compelled to be its own reward.

A similar argument can be brought against those who hold that the sole good is pleasure (or happiness, as some prefer to call it). This doctrine is regarded as self-evident by many, both philosophers and plain men. But although the general principle may at first sight seem obvious, many of its applications are highly paradoxical. To live in a fool's paradise is commonly considered a misfortune; yet in a world which allows no paradise of any other kind a fool's paradise is surely the happiest habitation. All hedonists are at great pains to prove that what are called the higher pleasures are really the more pleasurable. But plainly their anxiety to prove this arises from an uneasy instinct that such pleasures are higher, even if they are not more pleasurable. The bias which appears in hedonist arguments on this point is otherwise quite inexplicable. Although they hold that, 'quantity of pleasure being equal, pushpin is as good as poetry,' they are careful to argue that quantity of pleasure is *not* equal, but is greater in the case of poetry—a proposition which seems highly disputable, and chiefly commended by its edifying nature. Anyone would admit that the pleasure of poetry is a greater good than the pleasure of bathing on a hot day; but few people could say honestly that it is as intense. And even states of mind which, as a whole, are painful, may be highly good. Love of the dead may easily be the best thing in a life; yet it cannot but be full of pain. And conversely, we condemn pleasure derived from the love of what is bad; even if we admit that the pleasure in itself is a good, we consider the whole state of mind bad. If two bitter enemies lived in different countries, and each falsely believed that the other was undergoing tortures, each might feel pleasure; yet we should not consider such a state of things good. We should even think it much worse than a state in which each derived pain from the belief that the other was in torture. It may, of course, be said that this is due to the fact that hatred in general causes more pain than pleasure, and hence is condemned broadly on hedonistic grounds, without sufficient regard to possible exceptions. But the possibility of exceptions to the principle that hatred is bad can hardly be seriously maintained, except by a theorist in difficulties.

Thus while we may admit that all pleasure, in itself, is probably more or less good, we must hold that pleasures are not good in proportion to their intensity, and that many states of mind, although pleasure is an element in them, are bad as a whole, and may even be worse than they would be if the pleasure were absent. And this result has been reached by appealing to ethical judgments with which almost everyone would agree. I conclude, therefore, from all that has been adduced in this section, that although some ultimate ethical differences must be admitted between different people, by far the greater part of the commonly observed differences are due either to asking the wrong question (as, e.g., by mistaking means for ends), or to the influence of a hasty theory in falsifying immediate judgments. There is reason to hope, therefore, that a very large measure of agreement on ethical questions may be expected to result from clearer thinking; and this is probably the chief benefit to be ultimately derived from the study of ethics.

43. We may now sum up our whole discussion of ethics. The most fundamental notions in ethics, we agreed, are the notions of intrinsic good and evil. These are wholly independent of other notions, and the goodness or badness of a thing cannot be inferred from any of its other qualities, such as its existence or non-existence. Hence what actually occurs has no bearing on what ought to occur, and what ought to occur has no bearing on what does occur. The next pair of notions with which we were concerned were those of

objective right and wrong. The objectively right act is the act which a man will hold that he ought to perform when he is not mistaken. This, we decided, is that one, of all the acts that are possible, which will probably produce the best results. Thus in judging what actions are *right* we need to know what results are *good*. When a man is mistaken as to what is objectively right, he may nevertheless act in a way which is subjectively right; thus we need a new pair of notions, which we called *moral* and *immoral*. A moral act is virtuous and deserves praise; an immoral act is sinful and deserves blame. A moral act, we decided, is one which the agent would have judged right after an appropriate amount of candid reflection,[1] where the appropriate amount of reflection depends upon the difficulty and importance of his decision. We then considered the bearing of determinism on morals, which we found to consist in a limitation of the acts which are *possible* under any circumstances. If determinism is true, there is a sense in which no act is possible except the one which in fact occurs; but there is another sense, which is the one relevant to ethics, in which any act is possible which is contemplated during deliberation (provided it is *physically* possible, i.e. will be performed if we will to perform it). We then discussed various forms of egoism, and decided that all of them are false. Finally, we considered some mistakes which are liable to be made in attempting to form an immediate judgment as to the goodness or badness of a thing, and we decided that, when these mistakes are avoided, people probably differ very little in their judgments of intrinsic value. The making of such judgments we did not undertake; for if the reader agrees, he could make them himself, and if he disagrees without falling into any of the possible confusions, there is no way of altering his opinion.

[1] Or after a small amount in the case of acts which ought to be impulsive.

II

ON HISTORY[1]

Of all the studies by which men acquire citizenship of the intellectual commonwealth, no single one is so indispensable as the study of the past. To know how the world developed to the point at which our individual memory begins; how the religions, the institutions, the nations among which we live, became what they are; to be acquainted with the great of other times, with customs and beliefs differing widely from our own—these things are indispensable to any consciousness of our position, and to any emancipation from the accidental circumstances of our education. It is not only to the historian that history is valuable, not only to the professed student of archives and documents, but to all who are capable of a contemplative survey of human life. But the value of history is so multiform, that those to whom some one of its sides appeals with especial force are in constant danger of forgetting all the others.

I

History is valuable, to begin with, because it is true; and this, though not the whole of its value, is the foundation and condition of all the rest. That all knowledge, as such, is in some degree good, would appear to be at least probable; and the knowledge of every historical fact possesses this element of goodness, even if it possesses no other. Modern historians, for the most part, seem to regard truth as constituting the whole of the value of history. On this ground they urge the

[1] Reprinted from *The Independent Review*, July 1904.

self-effacement of the historian before the document; every intrusion of his own personality, they fear, will involve some degree of falsification. Objectivity before all things is to be sought, they tell us; let the facts be merely narrated, and allowed to speak for themselves—if they can find tongues. It follows, as a part of the position, that all facts are equally important; and, although this doctrine can never be quite conformed to in practice, it seems nevertheless to float before many minds as an ideal toward which research may gradually approximate.

That the writing of history should be based on the study of documents is an opinion which it would be absurd to controvert. For they alone contain evidence as to what really occurred; and it is plain that untrue history can have no great value. Moreover, there is more life in one document than in fifty histories (omitting a very few of the best); by the mere fact that it contains what belongs to that actual past time, it has a strangely vivid life-in-death, such as belongs to our own past when some sound or scent awakens it. And a history written after the event can hardly make us realize that the actors were ignorant of the future; it is difficult to believe that the late Romans did not know their empire was about to fall, or that Charles I was unaware of so notorious a fact as his own execution.

But if documents are, in so many ways, superior to any deliberate history, what function remains to the historian? There is, to begin with, the business of selection. This would be admitted by all; for the materials are so vast, that it is impossible to present the whole of them. But it is not always realized that selection involves a standard of value among facts, and therefore implies that truth is not the sole aim in recording the past. For all facts are equally true; and selection among them is only possible by means of some other criterion than their truth. And the existence of some such criterion is obvious; no one would maintain, for example, that the little Restoration scandals recorded by Grammont are as important as the letters on the Piedmontese massacres, by which Milton, in the name of Cromwell, summoned the tardy potentates of Europe.

It may be said, however, that the only true principle of selection is the purely scientific one; those facts are to be regarded as important which lead to the establishment of general laws. Whether there ever will be a science of history, it is quite impossible to guess; at any rate it is certain that no such science exists at present, except to some slight degree in the province of economics. In order that the scientific criterion of importance among facts should be applicable, it is necessary that two or more hypotheses should have been invented, each accounting for a large number of the facts; and that then a crucial fact should be discovered which discriminates between the rivals. Facts are important, in the inductive sciences, solely in relation to theories; and new theories give importance to new facts. So, for example, the doctrine of Natural Selection brought into prominence all transitional and intermediate species, the existence of rudiments, and the embryological record of descent. But it will hardly be maintained that history has reached, or is soon likely to reach, a point where such standards are applicable to its facts. History, considered as a body of truth, seems destined long to remain almost purely descriptive. Such generalizations as have been suggested—omitting the sphere of economics—are, for the most part, so plainly unwarranted as to be not even worthy of refutation. Burke argued that all revolutions end in military tyrannies, and predicted Napoleon. In so far as his argument was based on the analogy of Cromwell, it was a very lucky hit; but certainly not a scientific law. It is true that numerous instances are not always necessary to establish a law, provided the essential and relevant circumstances can be easily disentangled. But, in history, so many circumstances of a small and accidental nature are relevant, that no broad and simple uniformities are possible.

And there is a further point against this view of history as solely or chiefly a causal science. Where our main endeavour is to discover general laws, we regard these as intrinsically more valuable than any of the facts which they inter-connect. In astronomy, the law of gravitation is plainly better worth knowing than the position of a particular planet on a particular night, or even on every night throughout a year. There are in the law a splendour and simplicity and sense of mastery, which illuminate a mass of otherwise uninteresting details. And so again in biology: until the theory of evolution put meaning into the bewildering variety of organic structures, the particular facts were interesting only to the professed naturalist. But in history the matter is far otherwise. In economics, it is true, the data are often subordinate to the attempts at science which are based upon them; but in all other departments, the data are more interesting, and the scientific superstructure less satisfactory. Historical facts, many of them, have an intrinsic value, a profound interest on their own account, which makes them worthy of study, quite apart from any possibility of linking them together by means of causal laws.

The study of history is often recommended on the ground of its utility in regard to the problems of present-day politics. That history has great utility in this respect, it is impossible to deny; but it is necessary very carefully to limit and define the kind of guidance to be expected from it. The 'teachings of history', in the crude sense, pre-suppose the discovery of causal laws, usually of a very sweeping kind; and 'teachings' of this sort, though in certain cases they may do no harm, are always theoretically unsound. In the eighteenth century perpetually, and in our own day occasionally, arguments as to the value of liberty or democracy are drawn from Greece and Rome; their greatness or their decay, according to the bias of the author, is attributed to these causes. What can be more grotesque than to hear the rhetoric of the Romans applied to the circumstances of the French Revolution! The whole organization of a City State, based on slavery, without representative institutions, and without printing, is so utterly remote from any modern democracy as to make all analogy, except of the vaguest kind, totally frivolous and unreal. So with regard to imperialism, arguments are drawn from the successes and failures of the ancients. Shall we believe, for example, that Rome was ruined by the perpetual extension of her frontiers? Or shall we believe, with Mommsen, that the failure to conquer the Germans between the Rhine and the Danube was one of her most fatal errors? All such arguments will always be conducted according to the prejudices of the author; and all alike, even if they have some measure of truth in regard to the past, must be quite inapplicable to the present.

This evil is greatest when history is regarded as teaching some general philosophical doctrine, such as: Right, in the long run, is Might; Truth always prevails in the end; or, Progress is a universal law of society. All such doctrines require, for their support, a careful choice of place and time, and, what is worse, a falsification of values. A very flagrant instance of this danger is Carlyle. In the case of Puritanism, it led him to justify all Cromwell's acts of impatience and illegality, and arbitrarily to arrest his survey in 1658; how he accounted for the Restoration, it is impossible to say. In other cases, it led him still further astray. For it is often hard to discover on which side the Right lies, but the Might is visible to all men; thus the doctrine that Right is might slides insensibly into the belief that Might is Right. Hence the praise of Frederick and Napoleon and Bismarck, the pitiless contempt for the Negroes, the Irish, and the 'thirty-thousand distressed needlewomen'. In some such way, every general theory that all is for the best must be forced by the facts into defence of the indefensible.

Nevertheless, history has a function in regard to current affairs, but a function less direct, less exact, and less decisive. It may, in the first place, suggest minor maxims, whose truth, when they are once propounded, can be seen without the help of the events that suggested them. This is largely the case in economics, where most of the motives concerned are simple. It is the case also, for a similar reason, in regard to strategy. Wherever, out of the facts, a simple deductive argument from indubitable premises can be elicited, history may yield useful precepts. But these will only apply where the end is given, and are therefore of a technical nature. They can never tell the statesman what end to pursue, but only, within certain limits, how some of the more definite ends, such as wealth, or victory in war, are to be attained.

II

Another and a greater utility, however, belongs also to history. It enlarges the imagination, and suggests possibilities of action and feeling which would not have occurred to an uninstructed mind. It selects from past lives the elements which were significant and important; it fills our thoughts with splendid examples, and with the desire for greater ends than unaided reflection would have discovered. It relates the present to the past, and thereby the future to the present. It makes visible and living the growth and greatness of nations, enabling us to extend our hopes beyond the span of our own lives. In all these ways, a knowledge of history is capable of giving to statesmanship, and to our daily thoughts, a breadth and scope unattainable by those whose view is limited to the present.

What the past does for us may be judged, perhaps, by the consideration of those younger nations whose energy and enterprise are winning the envy of Europe. In them we see developing a type of man, endowed with all the hopefulness of the Renaissance or of the Age of Pericles, persuaded that his more vigorous efforts can quickly achieve whatever has proved too difficult for the generations that preceded him. Ignorant and contemptuous of the aims that inspired those generations, unaware of the complex problems that they attempted to solve, his rapid success in comparatively simple achievements encourages his confident belief that the future belongs to him. But to those who have grown up surrounded by monuments of men and deeds whose memory they cherish, there is a curious thinness about the thoughts and emotions that inspire this confidence; optimism seems to be sustained by a too exclusive pursuit of what can be easily achieved; and hopes are not transmuted into ideals by the habit of appraising current events by their relation to the history of the past. Whatever is different from the present is despised. That among those who contributed nothing to the dominion of Mammon great men lived, that wisdom may reside in those whose thoughts are not dominated by the machine, is incredible to this temper of mind. Action, Success, Change, are its watchwords; whether the action is noble, the success in a good cause, or the change an improvement in anything except wealth, are questions which there is no time to ask. Against this spirit, whereby all leisure, all care for the ends of life, are sacrificed to the struggle to be first in a worthless race, history and the habit of living with the past are the surest antidotes; and in our age, more than ever before, such antidotes are needed.

The record of great deeds is a defeat of Time; for it prolongs their power through many ages after they and their authors have been swallowed by the abyss of the non-existent. And, in regard to the past, where contemplation is not obscured by desire and the need for action, we see, more clearly than in the lives about us, the value, for good and evil, of the aims men have pursued and the means they have adopted. It is good, from time to time, to view the present as already past, and to examine what elements it contains that will add to the world's store of permanent possessions, that will live and give life when we and all our generation have perished. In the light of this contemplation, all human experience is transformed, and whatever is sordid or personal is purged away. And, as we grow in wisdom, the treasure-house of the ages opens to our view; more and more we learn to know and love the men through whose devotion all this wealth has become ours. Gradually, by the contemplation of great lives, a mystic communion becomes possible, filling the soul like music from an invisible choir. Still, out of the past, the voices of heroes call us. As, from a lofty promontory, the bell of an ancient cathedral, unchanged since the day when Dante returned from the kingdom of the dead, still sends its solemn warning across the waters, so their voice still sounds across the intervening sea of time; still, as then, its calm deep tones speak to the solitary tortures of cloistered aspiration, putting the serenity of things eternal in place of the doubtful struggle against ignoble joys and transient pleasures. Not by those about them were they heard; but they spoke to the winds of heaven, and the winds of heaven tell the tale to the great of later days. The great are not solitary; out of the night come the voices of those who have gone before, clear and courageous; and so through the ages they march, a mighty procession, proud, undaunted, unconquerable. To join in this glorious company, to swell the immortal paeon of those whom fate could not subdue—this may not be happiness; but what is happiness to those whose souls are filled with that celestial music? To them is given what is better than happiness: to know the fellowship of the great, to live in the inspiration of lofty thoughts, and to be illumined in every perplexity by the fire of nobility and truth.

But history is more than the record of individual men, however great: it is the province of history to tell the biography, not only of men, but of Man; to present the long procession of generations as but the passing thoughts of one continuous life; to transcend their blindness and brevity in the slow unfolding of the tremendous drama in which all play their part. In the migrations of races, in the birth and death of religions, in the rise and fall of empires, the unconscious units, without any purpose beyond the moment, have contributed unwittingly to the pageant of the ages; and, from the greatness of the whole, some breath of greatness breathes over all who participated in the march. In this lies the haunting power of the dim history beyond written records. There, nothing is known but the cloudy outlines of huge events; and, of all the separate lives that came and went, no memory remains. Through unnumbered generations, forgotten sons worshipped at the tombs of forgotten fathers, forgotten mothers bore warriors whose bones whitened the silent steppes of Asia. The clash of arms, the hatreds and oppressions, the blind conflicts of dumb nations, are all still, like a distant waterfall; but slowly, out of the strife, the nations that we know emerged, with a heritage of poetry and piety transmitted from the buried past.

And this quality, which is all that remains of pre-historic times, belongs also to the later periods where the knowledge of details is apt to obscure the movement of the whole. We, too, in all our deeds, bear our part in a process of which we cannot guess the development: even the obscurest are actors in a drama of which we know only that it is great. Whether any purpose that we value will be achieved, we cannot tell; but the drama itself, in any case, is full of Titanic grandeur. This quality it is the business of the historian to extract from the bewildering multitude of irrelevant details. From old books, wherein the loves, the hopes, the faiths of bygone generations lie embalmed, he calls pictures before our minds, pictures of high endeavours and brave hopes, living still through his care, in spite of failure and death. Before all is wrapped in oblivion, the historian must compose afresh, in each succeeding age, the epitaph upon the life of Man.

The past alone is truly real: the present is but a painful, struggling birth into the immutable being of what is no longer. Only the dead exist fully. The lives of the living are fragmentary, doubtful, and subject to change; but the lives of the dead are complete, free from the sway of Time, the all but omnipotent lord of the world. Their failures and successes, their hopes and fears, their joys and pains, have become eternal—our efforts cannot now abate one jot of them. Sorrows long buried in the grave, tragedies of which only a fading memory remains, loves immortalized by Death's hallowing touch—these have a power, a magic, an untroubled calm, to which no present can attain.

Year by year, comrades die, hopes prove vain, ideals fade; the enchanted land of youth grows more remote, the road of life more wearisome; the burden of the world increases, until the labour and the pain become almost too heavy to be borne; joy fades from the weary nations of the earth, and the tyranny of the future saps men's vital force; all that we love is waning, waning from the dying world. But the past, ever devouring the transient offspring of the present, lives by the universal death; steadily, irresistibly, it adds new trophies to its silent temple, which all the ages build; every great deed, every splendid life, every achievement and every heroic failure, is there enshrined. On the banks of the river of Time, the sad procession of human generations is marching slowly to the grave; in the quiet country of the Past, the march is ended, the tired wanderers rest, and all their weeping is hushed.

III

SCIENCE AND HYPOTHESIS[1]

In this book[2], which consists in the main of previous articles somewhat re-written, M. Poincaré's well-known merits appear to the full—his lucid and trenchant brevity, his air of easy mastery, which often makes his thought appear less profound than it is, and his power of co-ordinating the whole domain of mathematics and physics in a single system of ideas. But these merits, great as they are, are accompanied by what cannot but appear as defects to anyone accustomed to philosophy. His fundamental principles, as a rule, are assumed without discussion, presumably on the ground that they are self-evident, yet many of them are at the extreme of one side in time-honoured controversies. Such are: Deduction can never give new truth; mathematics, so far as it is not mere definition, derives its certainty from the fact that its principles concern not nature, but properties of the mind; science teaches us, not about things themselves, but about their relations; 'experiment is the sole source of truth. It alone can teach us something new; it alone can give us certainty.' There are also some principles embedded in the chapter on probability; but these are harder to discover or to state precisely.

The first section, on Number and Magnitude, begins with the question: If mathematics is not deductive, why is it rigorous? and if it is deductive, why is it not one vast

[1] Reprinted from *Mind,* July 1905.

[2] *Science and Hypothesis* by H. Poincaré, Member of the Institute of France. With a preface by J. Larmor, D.SC, Sec. R.S., Lucasian Professor of Mathematics in the University of Cambridge. London and Newcastle-on-Tyne: The Walter Scott Publishing Co. Ltd, 1905. Pp xxvii, 244.

tautology? The conclusion arrived at is that all pure mathematics depends upon mathematical induction—the principle, that is, that if a property belongs to the number 0, and also belongs to $n + 1$, whenever it belongs to n, then this property belongs to all the natural numbers. This principle may be expressed popularly by saying that we can get to any one of the natural numbers, starting from 0, by successive additions of 1 continued for a sufficient (finite) number of times. This principle, M. Poincaré says, enables mathematics to pass from the particular to the general; it condenses within itself an infinite number of syllogisms: it is synthetic *a priori* intuition; it affirms the power of the mind to conceive the indefinite repetition of the same act, when the act is once possible; it is 'necessarily imposed upon us, because it is only the affirmation of a property of the mind itself' (p. 13); yet 'this induction is only possible if the same operation can be repeated indefinitely' (p. 16).

Since the above theory of deduction underlies most of the later parts of the book, I shall consider it at some length. First of all, the meaning of mathematical induction according to M. Poincaré is far from clear. It affirms, we are told, that we can conceive the indefinite repetition of an act which is once possible. Yet it is not a mere repetition that is meant. What is affirmed is not (say) that if we can at one time add 1 to 2 then we can do so at another time; what is affirmed is that if we can add 1 to 2 and so get 3, we can add 1 to 3 and so get 4, and so on *ad infinitum*. That is, it is affirmed that if an operation transforms an object a into an object b, it can be performed on b so as to turn it into c: in better words, if a has the relation R to b then b will have the relation R to some term c. Now this property holds of some relations, but not of others;[1] hence M. Poincaré has to admit that induction is only possible if the same operation can be repeated indefinitely. Hence his *a priori* synthetic intuition becomes: 'If an operation is one of those than can be repeated indefinitely, then it is

---

[1] E.g. it is not the case that if a is the wife of b, b must be the wife of someone else.

capable of indefinite repetition.' It can hardly be this principle which saves mathematics from being a 'vast tautology'.

The fact is, of course, that M. Poincaré only means to apply his principle to the operation of adding 1 to a number. The property of the mind which is in question is, therefore, this: 'It is possible to add 1 to any number whatever.' But this does not yield us the principle of mathematical induction, which says not merely that the addition of 1 will always give a number, but that *every* natural number can be obtained by such additions starting from 0. It limits the natural numbers at the same time that it shows the series of them to be endless: they all appear in this series, any point of which can be reached by successive steps starting from 0. Now this limitation, which is what is really used when proofs are conducted by means of mathematical induction, is not a synthetic *a priori* intuition, or a property of the mimd, or a condensation of an infinite number of syllogisms; it is merely the *definition* of a *finite* number. A finite number means one to which mathematical induction applies; an infinite number means one to which it does not apply. There are infinite numbers, and many theorems can be proved concerning them, as well as concerning things which are not numbers at all; hence plainly mathematical induction is not what accounts for the fruitfulness of mathematics.

Again, M. Poincaré is mistaken in regarding mathematical induction as a means of passing from the particular to the general: it is merely a means of passing from one general proposition to another. Our premisses are, first, that a certain property belongs to 0; this, we may admit, is particular; second, that *every* finite number n is such that, if n has the said property, so has $n + 1$; this is general. The conclusion is that every finite number has the said property; but this conclusion has exactly the same degree of generality as our second premiss. The appearance of passing from particular to general arises only from neglect of our second premiss.

The notion that a principle is rendered certain by expressing a property of the mind is also curious. 'The mind' must be somebody's mind; all minds are a part of nature; minds differ from time to time and from person to person; and psychology is not usually considered more certain than arithmetic. M. Poincaré's view, like Kant's, assumes that we know already, before we have any other knowledge, that all minds are alike in certain respects; that their likeness consists in their all sharing certain beliefs; that these beliefs have no warrant except their universal existence, i.e. that they are universal delusions; and that universal delusions are what we call *a priori* truths, and as such are the indispensable premisses of all really indubitable knowledge.

M. Poincaré gives no reasons for the view that deduction can never give new truths. The fact is that the general principles of deduction are analogous, in this respect, to what he conceives mathematical induction to be; that is to say, they lead to conclusions which are other than themselves, so that in this sense they are synthetic. We shall conclude, therefore, that mathematics does not, as M. Poincaré affirms (p. 24), contain an inductive element, and yet is not 'a vast tautology'.

The second part, on Space, repeats the contention that none of the various Euclidean and non-Euclidean geometries is truer than another, but that the Euclidean is the most convenient. The argument is, that all our experiments concern *bodies*, and that any apparently non-Euclidean result can be interpreted as due to the nature of bodies, not to the nature of space. Admitting this, I do not think the consequence follows. In the first place, it does not follow that the Euclidean geometry must always remain the most convenient. But this point is of less importance than the following: There are relations which arrange the points of space in any order imaginable, e.g. so that objects which we perceive as near together would be widely separated, while objects which, in the perceived spatial order, are very distant, would come between objects which are very near to us. In short, relations subsist between points which make a complete re-arrangement of them, not at all resembling the arrangement we perceive. These other arrangements differ from the one we perceive, it would seem, just in the fact that we do not perceive them; and this brings out the necessity of supposing that the spatial relations we regard as actual *are* perceived. But if this is the case, then those relations constitute a Euclidean or some definite non-Euclidean space, though it may be impossible for us to know which. In any case, it is an empirical fact that the material parts of any ordinary object are nearer to each other than are the parts of two objects between which the said object lies, and that we do perceive bodies as made up of parts more or less contiguous. All this shows that matter is arranged by perception in a spatial order which is certainly different from some of the possible orders; and it is only for reasons whose origin is in perception that we select at all from among the orders that are *a priori* possible. And this suffices to prove that geometry is not *wholly* conventional, as M. Poincaré contends.

The third part, on Force, discusses rational mechanics, and finds that its principles also are really definitions. 'There is no escape,' we are told, 'from the following definition, which is only a confession of failure: *Masses are co-efficients which it is found convenient to introduce into calculations*' (p. 103). The discussion of which this is the conclusion is admirable. But it is admitted that the principles of mechanics were obtained, and ought to be obtained, by experiment, and this introduces an element which is not conventional. The view advocated seems to be that actual bodies behave in a way very like the way in which the ideal bodies of rational mechanics behave, but that the principles of mechanics are rendered conventional by the fact that, whenever they might seem to be violated, we prefer to invent hypothetical bodies or hypothetical motions which prevent the violation. Thus a principle, it would seem, becomes conventional the moment we are less willing to abandon it than to seek a supplementary hypothesis to preserve it. It is possible, however—though M. Poincaré takes no account of the possibility—to believe that such a principle is strictly true, and that any supplementary hypothesis which may be necessary to preserve it is thereby proved to be also true. M. Poincaré ignores such a view, because it leads to the result that a law may be true although experiment can neither prove nor disprove it. The course of science seems to be, that a general principle is found to account for a number of phenomena, while others, though not inconsistent with it, are not to be explained by it without further hypotheses. In every subsequent experiment, as M. Poincaré points out, no one hypothesis is really being tested, but a whole body of hypotheses; and if any one of them is regarded as beyond doubt, it will almost always be possible to explain a phenomenon by denying one or more of the other hypotheses. Hence a hypothesis which we no longer regard as open to doubt is thereby withdrawn from the region of experimental verification; but it does not follow that such a hypothesis is a mere convention. Indeed, if it did, mere completeness of proof would constitute disproof.

There is an unsatisfactory chapter on absolute and relative motion, in which it is admitted that, from Foucault's pendulum, from the flattening of the earth at the poles, and from the different weights of a given mass in different latitudes, it would be possible to infer the rotation of the earth even if the sky were always cloudy and we saw no heavenly bodies. It follows that the rotation of the earth would be convenient as accounting for the phenomena even if there were no heavenly bodies; but this involves absolute rotation, and is therefore meaningless, in M. Poincaré's opinion. He says (p. 117): 'This affirmation, "the earth turns round", has no meaning, since it cannot be verified by experiment . . . or, in other words, these two propositions, "the earth turns round," and "it is more convenient to suppose that the earth turns round," have one and the same meaning.' But if "the earth turns round" has no meaning, it has the same meaning as "Abracadabra", and therefore, if M. Poincaré is right, it has the same meaning as "it is more convenient to suppose that Abracadabra". But M. Poincaré supposes it true that it is more convenient to suppose the earth turns round; yet I cannot see what convenience is going to result from supposing

Abracadabra. In short, what it is convenient to suppose must have some meaning; hence, it would seem, the facts which make it convenient to suppose that the earth turns round prove that there is such a thing as absolute rotation.

The fourth and last part, on Nature, deals with physics, and points out where, according to M. Poincaré, the domain of convention and definition ceases, and substantial scientific laws come into play. There is an interesting comparison of the methods of English and French physicists, giving the preference, in the main, to the former as more experimental and less concerned to rear a logical edifice. There is also an interesting but unsatisfactory discussion of probability, whose importance, in inductive proofs, M. Poincaré very justly emphasizes, though this discussion is rather marred, logically, by the assumption that, in the long run, the most probable distribution, say of heads and tails, will actually occur (p. 188), whereas we can only say that it will *probably* occur. But I pass by these matters to consider the main theses of this part, which are two: (1) that science deals only with the *relations* of things; (2) that experiment is the sole test of truth.

(1) Questions concerning the real, as opposed to the relation of real things, are said to be illusory and devoid of meaning (pp. xxiv, 163). Certainly we have much more belief in the accuracy of our perceptions of relations than in that of our perceptions of qualities. When we see green in one place and red in another, we are willing to believe that secondary qualities are subjective, but not that the fact of difference between what is in the two places is an illusion. It is only by holding fast to relations as perceived that science manages, on an empirical basis, to construct a world so different from that of perception. Why we should trust in our perception of relations I do not know; but it is a fact that we do so. But I do not see how it can be maintained that questions as to the qualities of real things are *unmeaning*. The proposition amounts to this, that if *a* really exists, a statement about *a* has no *meaning* unless it asserts a relation to a *b* which also really

exists. The fact seems to be, not that such propositions are unmeaning, but that, except in psychology, they are unknowable. We may even push the theory further, and say that in general even the relations are for the most part unknown, and what is known are properties of the relations, such as are dealt with by mathematics. And this, I think, expresses substantially the same view as that which M. Poincaré really holds.

(2) That experiment alone can teach us something new, is a view underlying all M. Poincaré's theories, and is connected with his opinion that deductions are mere tautologies. Yet he himself admits that a good experiment teaches more than an isolated fact (p. 142), and that 'the physicist who would content himself with experiment pure and simple would be compelled to enunciate very extraordinary laws indeed' (p. 143). But it is surely plain that if experiment were the *sole* source of truth, no experiment could teach anything beyond itself. To do this, the result of the experiment must imply other propositions, and this implication, in the long run, cannot itself be wholly proved by experiment. We speak of general laws being proved by experiment, but the mere fact of their generality shows that they are not *wholly* proved by experiment, since all experience is of particulars. When a general law is proved by experiment, it is merely selected by experiment from among several, which are themselves regarded *a priori* as the only possible laws. M. Poincaré more or less admits that the uniformity of nature and other fundamental principles cannot be *proved* by experiment; but he concludes that they are only probable. His argument in favour of their being even probable depends, however, upon assumptions as to probability—notably that an observed regularity is not likely to be due to accident—which are certainly incapable of experimental proof, or of being made probable without some axiom concerning probability.

The book throughout is interesting, and has the great merit of making its meaning perfectly definite. Moreover, M. Poincaré's opinions, whether one agrees or disagrees, are such as it is by no means easy to disprove, and the disproof, when it is possible, is instructive. Professor Larmor's introduction suggests that its author feels a strong objection to M. Poincaré's scepticism, but this scepticism is never wanton, and has always a constructive purpose. I cannot but think that the translator has sometimes misplaced a negative; e.g. on page 48, 'these geometries of Riemann . . . can never be . . . purely analytical' surely does not translate 'ne peuvent jamais être que', which means 'can never be more than'. Similar mistakes seem to occur on pages 18, 162, 205.

IV

PRAGMATISM[1]

The appearance in the world of a genuinely new philosophy is at all times an event of very great importance. More particularly is this the case when the new philosophy embodies the prevailing temper of the age better than any of its older rivals; for in that case it is likely to establish itself in popular favour, to colour the thoughts of the educated and half-educated public, and to strengthen those elements in the mental atmosphere to which it owes its success. It would be a mistake to suppose that new philosophies are always adapted to the age in which they appear; but when they are not, they fail to win wide acceptance whatever their other merits may be. Spinoza, for example, deserved success as well as Leibniz; yet his works were almost wholly neglected until more than a century after his death, because the political and intellectual *milieu* was not one in which they could thrive. Leibniz, on the contrary, gave scope to the love of calculation which men derived from the discoveries of his time, and represented the world as a hierarchy of systems, each exactly like the Holy Roman Empire; his system, therefore, ruled the German mind until the ferment which preceded the French Revolution set men's thoughts running in new channels.

The philosophy which is called *Pragmatism* or *Humanism*[2] is genuinely new, and is singularly well adapted to the predominant intellectual temper of our time. As regards its adaptation to the age, we shall have more to say when we

[1] Reprinted from the *Edinburgh Review*, April 1909.
[2] These two names are distinguished by William James and Dr Schiller in various ways at various times. For our purposes, it is unnecessary to consider these distinctions.

have considered what it is. As regards novelty, its authors show a modesty which, in our opinion, is somewhat excessive. 'Pragmatism, a new name for some old ways of thinking', William James calls his book; and Dr Schiller constantly asserts that his doctrines are those of Protagoras. As for Protagoras, we know sufficiently little about him to be able to read into him almost any doctrine we please; and the appeal to him may be regarded as mainly due to the desire to produce an ancestry which has acquired respectability by the lapse of time. With regard to more modern precursors, it must be admitted that many philosophers—as chief among whom we may mention Nietzsche—have paved the way for the new doctrines. Nevertheless the cardinal point in the pragmatist philosophy, namely, its theory of truth, is so new, and so necessary to the rest of the philosophy, even to those parts which had been previously maintained by others, that its inventors cannot be regarded as merely developing the thoughts of less explicit predecessors.

The name 'pragmatism' was first invented by Mr C. S. Peirce, as long ago as 1878. It was applied by him to the doctrine that the significance of a thought lies in the actions to which it leads. In order to estimate the difference between two different beliefs about the same matter, he maintained we ought to consider what difference in conduct would result according as we adopted the one belief or the other. If no difference would result, the two beliefs are not effectively different. Mr Peirce's doctrine, however, remained sterile until it was taken up twenty years later by William James, who, while retaining the word 'pragmatism', gave it a more sweeping significance. The full-fledged philosophy is to be attributed to him and Dr Schiller jointly. Professor Dewey, of Columbia University, is also to be reckoned among the founders of pragmatism. His writings are more technical and less popular than those of James and Dr Schiller, but on certain points his exposition is perhaps preferable to theirs.[1]

[1] Cf. especially an article on 'The Experimental Theory of Knowledge', *Mind*, N.S., No. 59 (July 1906).

PRAGMATISM

As an introduction to pragmatism, it is interesting to read William James's essay on 'The Will to Believe', first published in 1896, and reprinted in book form in the following year. In this essay, though the word 'pragmatism' does not appear, we find much that is characteristic of James's later views. The thesis he is advocating is that, in certain cases, it is right to believe whole-heartedly in one of two alternatives, even when there is no evidence as to which of them is true. These cases arise, he says, when we are compelled to choose between two hypotheses, each of which seems to us possible, and when it makes a great difference which we choose. The instances he has in mind are chiefly questions of morals and religion. In a moral perplexity we are compelled to come to some decision, since inaction is as much a decision as action. In regard to religion, also, we must act as though it were true or as though it were false; we are therefore practically compelled to choose. His contention is that, in such cases, it would be foolish to refuse to have faith merely on the ground that we do not find conclusive evidence on either side of the question. To quote his own words:

> Our passional nature not only lawfully may, but must, decide an option between propositions, whenever it is a genuine option that cannot by its nature be decided on intellectual grounds; for to say, under such circumstances, 'Do not decide, but leave the question open', is itself a passional decision—just like deciding yes or no—and is attended with the same risk of losing the truth.

He proceeds to justify himself against the charge of insufficient regard for truth, not, as he would do now, by contending that, in the absence of other evidence, the answer which gives the greatest emotional satisfaction *is* true, but on a variety of grounds tending to show that there are no sufficient moral arguments against *thinking* it true. He points out, to begin with, that emotions and wishes, though often unable to alter our beliefs when these have become established, nevertheless play a great part in initially deciding what our beliefs are to be. He points out next that our duty in the matter of opinion has two branches: (i) we must know the truth; (ii) we must avoid error. These two precepts, he says, have very different results. If, in cases where evidence is lacking, we abstain wholly from either belief, we are sure of not incurring error, but, on the other hand, we are sure of not knowing truth. If, however, we decide for one of the alternatives, we have an even chance of knowing the truth. It follows that those who urge us to abstain from belief in the absence of evidence consider it more important to avoid error than to believe truth. This 'horror of being duped' he represents as a somewhat contemptible form of cowardice; 'our errors', he says, 'are surely not such awfully solemn things. In a world where we are so certain to incur them in spite of all our caution, a certain lightness of heart seems healthier than this excessive nervousness on their behalf.' The legitimate conclusion from this argument would be that, in such cases as William James has in mind, we ought to believe both alternatives; for in that case we are sure of 'knowing' the truth in the matter. If it were said that to believe both is a psychological impossibility, we would rejoin that, on the contrary, it is often done, and that those who cannot yet do it need only practise the 'will to believe' until they have learnt to believe that the law of contradiction is false—a feat which is by no means as difficult as it is often supposed to be.

William James proceeds to point out that, in the case of religion, the choice between believing and disbelieving possesses all the characteristics of the options which, according to him, ought to be decided by the emotions. He tacitly assumes that there is no evidence for or against religion, and he points out that by refusing either to believe or to disbelieve we lose the benefits of religion just as much as by deciding to disbelieve.

Scepticism, then, is not avoidance of option; it is option of a certain kind of risk. *Better risk loss of truth than chance of error*—that is your faith-vetoer's exact position. He is actively playing his stake as much as the believer is; he is backing the field against the religious hypothesis, just as the believer is backing the religious hypothesis against the field. . . . It is not intellect against all passions, then; it is only intellect with one passion laying down its law. And by what, forsooth, is the supreme wisdom of this passion warranted? Dupery for dupery, what proof is there that dupery through hope is so much worse than dupery through fear?

The conclusion is that, although there is no evidence in favour of religion, we ought nevertheless to believe it if we find satisfaction in so doing.

This essay on the will to believe is important, because it has been widely read and much criticized, both adversely and favourably, and because it affords a good introduction to the pragmatist temper of mind. Some practice in the will to believe is an almost indispensable preliminary to the acceptance of pragmatism; and conversely pragmatism, when once accepted, is found to give the full justification of the will to believe. We shall therefore, before proceeding to pragmatism proper, consider briefly what there is to be said, on a common-sense basis, against the doctrines so persuasively set forth in this essay.

We may observe, to begin with, the agnostic hypothesis upon which the whole argument rests. The hypothesis is that no evidence for or against religion is at present known. Pragmatists pose as the friends of religion (except in Italy), and many religious people have accepted them as allies. It is therefore worth while to emphasize this underlying hypothesis, and to point out the very questionable wisdom of accepting it as the basis of a defence of orthodoxy. With the truth or falsehood of this hypothesis, however, we need not concern ourselves in this discussion; the question for us is whether, granting the hypothesis, we can accept the results which William James derives from it.

Let us observe, in the first place, a confusion which runs

through the whole pragmatist account of knowledge, namely, the confusion between acting on an hypothesis and believing it. In the cases which William James has in mind, the option between rival hypotheses is, he says, a 'forced' option; i.e. it is not avoidable:

> If I say, 'Either accept this truth or go without it', I put on you a forced option, for there is no standing place outside of the alternative.

This statement appears to us to be contrary to many of the plainest facts of daily life. If, in walking along a country road, I come to a fork where there is no signpost and no passer-by, I have, from the point of view of action, a 'forced' option. I must take one road or other if I am to have any chance of reaching my destination; and I may have no evidence whatever as to which is the right road. I then *act* on one or other of the two possible hypotheses, until I find someone of whom I can ask the way. But I do not *believe* either hypothesis. My action is either right or wrong, but my belief is neither, since I do not entertain either of the two possible beliefs. The pragmatist assumption that I believe the road I have chosen to be the right one is erroneous. To infer belief from action, in the crude way involved in the assumption that we must 'either accept this truth or go without it', is to ignore the plain fact that our actions are constantly based upon probabilities, and that, in all such cases, we neither accept a truth nor go without it, but entertain it as an hypothesis. This applies, in particular, to the working hypotheses of science. A man of science who considers it worth while to devise experimental tests of an hypothesis, and to construct elaborate theories which use the hypothesis, is not on that account to be regarded as *believing* the hypothesis. Pragmatists tell us that, in such cases, the initial unverified *belief* is a necessary condition for the subsequent established theory, and by so doing they make out a case for the usefulness of believing before we have evidence. This is, however, a mistaken analysis of the state of mind of a man who is testing an hypothesis. All that is required, and all that occurs among careful investigators, is the belief that the hypothesis has a greater or smaller chance of being true, and for this belief there is probably sufficient evidence. The actual belief that the hypothesis *is* true, when it occurs, is apt to be a hindrance, since it retards the abandonment of false hypotheses when the evidence goes against them, and if the belief is general, it makes people regard experimental verification as unnecessary. The Aristotelians who opposed Galileo and refused to give weight to his experiments had faithfully obeyed the precepts revived by William James.

The matter is, however, more complicated in such cases as religious beliefs, where the chief benefit is derived from the emotional satisfaction of the belief itself, not from the useful actions to which it directly prompts. But here, too, the antithesis of 'accepting' or 'going without' is far too crude; we may regard the belief as more or less probable, entertain a greater or less degree of hope that it may be true, and derive, accordingly, a greater or less proportion of the comfort we should derive from complete belief. In practice, to adopt the pragmatists' test, the effect of partial belief is very different from that of complete belief. Complete belief, if the issue is sufficiently momentous, will justify persecution—assuming, as history warrants us in doing, that the blood of Protestant martyrs is the seed of the Catholic Church. An incomplete belief, on the contrary, will not warrant the infliction of an indubitable evil for the sake of a gain which may possibly be illusory. This affords a pragmatic argument against conceding *full* belief in such cases as those with which William James is concerned. But if, as he assumes, there is a genuine possibility of the truth of an hypothesis, it is in accordance with all the strictest tenets of scientific veracity that we should bear the hypothesis in mind, and allow to it whatever influence over our emotions and actions corresponds to the degree of its probability.

We will next examine the argument that, in doubtful cases, the precept 'we must know the truth' should lead us to believe one hypothesis at a venture, since, if we believe neither, we certainly do not know the truth. This argument rests upon an ambiguity in the word 'know'. At first sight it might be thought that if we believe what is in fact true we must have knowledge. But this is not the sense in which the word is commonly used. Suppose, to take a trivial instance, that a man believed that the late Prime Minister's name began with a B, but believed this because he thought Mr Balfour was the late Prime Minister. What he believes is in fact true, yet no one would say that he 'knew' that the late Prime Minister's name began with a B. In this case the true belief is based upon a false reason. But the case is similar when the true belief is based upon no reason (except, indeed, in the case of immediate data such as the facts of perception). Thus if, in the case of an option which we have no rational means of deciding, we believe one alternative at a venture, we cannot be said to *know*, even if, by good luck, we have chosen the alternative which in fact is true. In such cases, we cannot *know* the truth, though we may by chance *believe* it. Hence the precept 'we must know the truth', which James invokes, is irrelevant to the issue. The usual antitheses of belief and disbelief, what is known and what is unknown, are not adequate to meet the situation. The true precept of veracity, which includes both the pursuit of truth and the avoidance of error, is this: 'We ought to give to every proposition which we consider as nearly as possible that degree of credence which is warranted by the probability it acquires from the evidence known to us.' The further questions, what propositions to consider, and how much trouble to take to acquire knowledge of the evidence, depend of course upon our circumstances and the importance of the issue. But to go about the world believing everything in the hope that thereby we shall believe as much truth as possible is like practising polygamy in the hope that among so many we shall find someone who will make us happy.

Another interesting point to observe in James's doctrine is the immense multiplicity of differing beliefs which it simultaneously justifies in different people. This arises from the condition that the option must be what he calls a 'living' option, that is, it must be one in which either alternative seems to us possible.

> If I say to you: 'Be a theosophist or be a Mohammedan', it is probably a dead option, because for you neither hypothesis is likely to be alive. But if I say: 'Be an agnostic or be a Christian', it is otherwise: trained as you are, each hypothesis makes some appeal, however small, to your belief.

He points out that to different people different options are living. It follows that the beliefs which, on his principles, different men ought to adopt, are different, since the three conditions for adopting a belief without evidence are that the option should be *living, forced,* and *momentous.* One gathers (perhaps wrongly) from his instances that a Frenchman ought to believe in Catholicism, an American in the Monroe Doctrine, and an Arab in the Mahdi (he wrote before the battle of Omdurman). It seems odd that, in view of this outcome, he should maintain that acceptance of his doctrine would diminish persecution; for an essential part of each of the above three creeds is that people who think otherwise must be taught their place.

To sum up our criticism of 'The Will to Believe': It ignores the distinction between believing and entertaining an hypothesis, and wrongly assumes that if we do not completely believe an hypothesis, we must either completely disbelieve it or wholly suspend judgment. Hence it is able to represent the option 'Either accept this truth or go without it' as one from which there is no escape, whereas all experiment, both in science and in daily life, implies a state of mind which accepts neither alternative. He assumes that we may be said to 'know' a truth, when we believe it at a venture, without reasons, and that therefore, in order to maximize our knowledge, we have only to maximize our beliefs. And his doctrines lead to the conclusion that different people ought to have incompatible beliefs. These objections, we shall find, may also be urged against full-fledged pragmatism. But we must now approach somewhat more difficult topics than those which have concerned us hitherto, since pragmatism cannot be understood without examining its doctrine as to the nature of truth. To this doctrine, therefore, we will now turn our attention.

The pragmatic theory of truth takes credit to itself—rightly, as we think—for a due consideration of error. Most theories as to the nature of truth have tacitly assumed to begin with that all our beliefs are true, and have arrived at results incompatible with the existence of error. They have then had to add a postscript explaining that what we call error is really partial truth. If we think it is Tuesday when it is really Wednesday, we are at least right in thinking that 'it' is a day of the week. If we think America was discovered in 1066, we are at least right in thinking that something important happened in that year. If we think Charles I died in his bed, we are at least so far right that, in view of the many people who do die in their beds, he probably had the potentiality of dying in his bed. And so on. Dr Schiller rightly points to the *Theaetetus* as showing the difficulties to which a theory of knowledge is reduced by neglecting to take due account of error from the beginning; and among more recent books, Mr Joachim's *The Nature of Truth* is used to point the same moral.

Pragmatism, then, emphasizes from the start the fact that some of our beliefs turn out to be mistaken, and that the proper business of a theory of truth is to show how truth and falsehood are distinguished. This might seem, to those not sophisticated by philosophy, to be an obvious truism; but in fact philosophy has always regarded it as its business to prove (as far as possible) that everything is true, rather than to distinguish between truth and falsehood. Similarly in ethics, philosophers have not sought to distinguish between the good and the bad, so much as to prove that everything is good. If little truth has been attained in philosophy, the reason is chiefly that few philosophers have wished to attain truth.

Whether pragmatists are superior in this respect we shall not venture to pronounce; but at any rate the peculiarity of their bias makes them willing to admit facts which other philosophers find inconvenient, and among such facts is the prevalence of error.

In order to discover the difference between truth and falsehood, pragmatism sets about a Socratic inductive inquiry as to the things we call 'true' and 'false'. These words, to begin with, are applied to beliefs, and are applied only when a question has arisen. Concerning the ordinary facts of perception, we do not ask questions until we have become philosophers; we do not apply either of the words 'true' and 'false' to such unquestioned matters. But when once the question has arisen concerning some actual belief, 'Is it a true or a false belief?' how do we in fact decide the question? The answer of pragmatism is that if the belief furthers the purpose which led us to ask the question it is regarded as a 'true' belief; if it fails to further the purpose it is regarded as a 'false' belief. This, therefore, according to pragmatism, is the meaning of the words 'true' and 'false'. 'True' means 'furthering the purpose which led to the question'. Or, more explicitly: When, in pursuing any purpose, a belief is entertained which is relevant to the purpose, the belief is 'true' if it furthers the achievement of the purpose, and 'false' if it does not do so.[1]

A few quotations will serve to amplify and elucidate the above brief statement. After explaining recent changes in the methodology of science, James says:

Riding now on the front of this wave of scientific logic, Messrs Schiller and Dewey appear with their pragmatistic account of what truth everywhere signifies. Everywhere, these teachers say, 'truth' in our ideas and beliefs means the same thing that it means in science. It means, they say, nothing but this, *that ideas (which themselves are but parts of our*

---

[1] Cf. Schiller, *Studies in Humanism*, p. 154.

experience) become true just in so far as they help us to get into satisfactory relations with other parts of our experience.[1]

Again:

I am well aware how odd it must seem to some of you to hear me say that an idea is 'true' so long as to believe it is profitable to our lives. That it is *good*, for as much as it profits, you will gladly admit.... But is it not a strange mis-use of the word 'truth', you will say, to call ideas also 'true' for this reason? . . . You touch here upon the very central point of Messrs Schiller's, Dewey's and my own doctrine of truth. . . . Let me now say only this, that truth is *one species of good*, and not, as is usually supposed, a category distinct from good, and co-ordinate with it. *The true is the name of whatever proves itself to be good in the way of belief, and good, too, for definite assignable reasons.*[2]

The sixth of William James's lectures on pragmatism is concerned wholly with the notion of truth. He begins by assenting to the dictionary definition that 'truth' means 'the agreement' of our ideas with 'reality'. But, as he justly observes, this definition does not take us very far, unless we know what we mean by 'agreement' and what we mean by 'reality'. The pragmatist holds that different sorts of 'agree-ment' and different sorts of 'reality' are concerned in differ-ent cases. The popular notion that a true idea must copy its reality holds good, he says, of sensible things, but goes wrong as soon as we come to abstractions. The idea of the elasticity of a spring, for example, cannot, according to him, be a copy of a reality—presumably on the ground that an elasticity is not an actually existing thing. The question is, then, what sort of agreement with reality is possible in such cases? 'The great assumption of the intellectualists', he says, 'is that truth means essentially an inert static relation.' An *intellectualist*, by the way, is anyone who is not a pragmatist. He proceeds:

[1] *Pragmatism*, pp. 57, 58.
[2] Ibid., pp. 75, 76.

Pragmatism, on the other hand, asks its usual question. 'Grant an idea or belief to be true,' it says, 'what concrete difference will its being true make in anyone's actual life? How will the truth be realized? What experiences will be different from those which would obtain if the belief were false? What, in short, is the truth's cash-value in experiential terms?'

The moment pragmatism asks this question it sees the answer: *True ideas are those that we can assimilate, validate, corroborate and verify. False ideas are those that we cannot.* . . .

The truth of an idea is not a stagnant property inherent in it. Truth *happens* to an idea. It *becomes* true, is *made* true by events. Its verity *is* in fact an event, a process: the process namely of its verifying itself, its veri-*fication*. Its validity is the process of its valid-*ation*.[1]

Recurring to the definition of 'truth' as 'agreement with reality', James sums up by distinguishing three kinds of reality: (1) concrete facts, (2) 'abstract kinds of things and relations perceived intuitively between them', (3) truths already in our possession. 'Agreement' he defines as follows:

To 'agree' in the widest sense with a reality *can only mean to be guided either straight up to it or into its surroundings, or to be put into such working touch with it as to handle either it or something connected with it better than if we disagreed.* (p. 212.)

Two further quotations will complete the material required for understanding James's account of truth.

'*The true*', *to put it very briefly, is only the expedient in the way of our thinking, just as 'the right' is only the expedient in the way of our behaving.* Expedient in almost any fashion; and expedient in the long run and on the whole of course. (p. 222.)

Our account of truth is an account of truths in the plural, of processes of leading, realized *in rebus*, and having only this quality in common, that they *pay*. (p. 218.)

[1] *Pragmatism*, pp. 200, 201.

Before proceeding further, it will be as well to clear up a misunderstanding, from which the pragmatists themselves appear not to be exempt. When it is said that truth is 'one species of good', it is natural to suppose that ethical considerations are involved, and that logic will become dependent upon ethics. This view is, in fact, adopted in Dr Schiller's essay[1] on 'the ethical basis of metaphysics'. But a closer examination shows that pragmatists mean by the word 'good' whatever satisfies desire.[2] So far as we know, they have nowhere justified this use of the word, but that is not our present concern. What concerns us at present is to observe that, in virtue of this definition, only psychological considerations are relevant where, to judge from the language, ethical considerations might seem to be involved. In order to judge whether a belief is true, it is only necessary to discover whether it tends to the satisfaction of desire.[3] The nature of the desire to be satisfied is only relevant in so far as it may involve conflict with other desires. Thus psychology is paramount, not only over logic and the theory of knowledge, but also over ethics. In order to discover what is good, we have only to inquire how people are to get what they want; and 'true' beliefs are those which help in this process. This is the pragmatist theory of truth; and its consequences, as might be supposed, are far-reaching.

Before considering the metaphysic which Dr Schiller has deduced from the pragmatist theory of truth, let us examine the grounds upon which that theory is based. Most philoso-

---

[1] The first essay in his *Humanism*.

[2] Schiller, *Studies in Humanism*, p. 152: 'Good and bad also (in their wider and primary sense) have reference to purpose. "Good" is what conduces to, "bad" what thwarts, a purpose.'

[3] Schiller, *Studies in Humanism*, p. 154: 'In all actual knowing the question whether an assertion is "true" or "false" is decided uniformly and very simply. It is decided, that is, by its consequences, by its bearing on the interest which prompted to the assertion, by its relation to the purpose which put the question. To add to this that the consequences must be *good* is superfluous. For if and so far as an assertion satisfies or forwards the purpose of the inquiry to which it owes its being, it is so far "true"; if and so far as it thwarts or baffles it, it is unworkable, unserviceable, "false".'

phies are determined by their initial questions, and by the facts which habitually fill the imagination of the philosopher. The initial question of pragmatism is: What characteristics of beliefs do in fact lead men to regard some as true, others as false? The answer to this question—so pragmatism assumes—will give us the meaning of truth and falsehood. The facts which fill the imaginations of pragmatists are psychical facts: where others might think of the starry heavens, pragmatists think of the perception of the starry heavens; where others might think of God, pragmatists think of the belief in God, and so on. In discussing the sciences, they never think, like scientific specialists, about the facts upon which scientific theories are based: they think about the theories themselves. Thus their initial question and their habitual imaginative background are both psychological. In order to arrive at an external world, they have to prove that the belief in an external world has the marks which (according to them) distinguish a true belief. Hence they infer that there is an external world. And a similar process is necessary as regards all other facts which transcend the Ego.

One of the approaches to pragmatism is through the consideration of induction and scientific method. The old inductive philosophy, as exemplified in Mill's logic, conceived the nature and scope of induction far too narrowly, and pragmatism deserves credit for having remedied this defect. Induction, though it cannot give complete certainty, underlies all the sciences, even pure mathematics. In any science, we have a collection of facts bound together (as far as possible) by general laws. The facts appear, in the formal exposition, as deductions from the laws; this, at least, holds for the most advanced sciences, such as mathematics and physics. But in reality the laws are inductions from the facts. We cannot say that this or that fact proves this or that law: the whole body of facts proves (or, rather, renders probable) the whole body of laws. It might be thought that, in an *experimentum crucis*, a single fact establishes a single law; but this is only the case so long as the other laws of the science are taken for granted. If other facts should lead us to doubt the other laws, the interpretation of our *experimentum crucis* might be wholly changed. Thus the justification of a science is that it fits all the known facts, and that no alternative system of hypotheses is known which fits the facts equally well. We may therefore say truly that scientific theories are adopted simply because they *work*, i.e. because their consequences are satisfactory. Thus it would appear as though a right analysis of scientific induction led us straight to the pragmatic test of truth.

Certain objections to this conclusion, however, at once suggest themselves. In the first place, scientific induction assumes certain data, the 'facts' with which our theories have to agree. That the heavenly bodies have the apparent positions, in the sky, which we perceive them to have, is not proved by astronomy, but is assumed as the datum upon which astronomy proceeds. It would seem, therefore, that there are truths of fact which are prior to the whole inductive procedure, and that these truths of fact must be 'true' in some other sense than that the consequences of supposing them true are satisfactory. To this argument pragmatists reply that what really is 'fact' is neither true nor false, but prior to the whole antithesis of truth and falsehood. 'Day follows day, and its contents are simply added. The new contents themselves are not true, they simply *come* and *are*. Truth is *what we say about* them, and when we say that they have come, truth is satisfied by the plain additive formula.'[1] Pragmatists contend, therefore, that the mere recognition of facts is the simplest case of the application of their formula. If all 'truth' were of this simple nature, the pragmatist doctrine would be unnecessary, though there would be nothing to show that it was false. But the 'truths' which do not consist in the mere recognition of facts cannot, according to pragmatism, be explained in this simple way; hence we are forced to adopt a theory of truth not derived from the exclusive consideration of this simplest case. For the moment let us allow this

[1] James, *Pragmatism*, p. 62.

answer to pass. We shall return to the subject of 'facts' in connection with Dr Schiller's doctrine of the making of reality.

A more serious objection to the argument from the procedure of the sciences is derived from the ambiguity of the conception of 'working'. What science requires of a working hypothesis is that it shall work *theoretically*, i.e. that all its verifiable consequences shall be *true*, and none *false*. The law of gravitation enables us to calculate the motions of the heavenly bodies: so far as these motions can be observed, they are found to agree with our calculations. It is *true* that the heavenly bodies have such and such apparent positions at such and such times, and the law of gravitation agrees with this *truth*. This is what we mean when we say that the law 'works'. We do not mean that it gives us emotional satisfaction, that it satisfies our aspirations, that it is a help in navigation, or that it facilitates a virtuous life. Any or all of these may be true, but they are irrelevant; if they were all false, we should still say that the law 'works', because it agrees with observed facts. Thus the kind of 'working' which science desiderates is a very different thing from the kind which pragmatism considers to be the essence of truth.

To this, as to our previous objection, pragmatists reply that the 'truth' concerned is a particular species of 'truth', and that scientific working is a particular species of their general conception of working. Our purpose, they say, in asking the question to which the law of gravitation is an answer, is to be able to calculate the motions of the heavenly bodies. The law of gravitation furthers this purpose, and is therefore true in the pragmatic sense. This answer shows that the procedure of science, so far, has not been shown to *contradict* pragmatism; but it does not show that the procedure of science positively supports pragmatism. Where, as in science, our purpose is to discover truth, an answer which furthers our purpose will be true. But from this truism it cannot be inferred (as pragmatists pretend) that if we had had some quite different purpose, an answer which furthered it would still have been true. Another objection to the argument from 'working hypotheses' is that by men of science these are explicitly contrasted with established truths. An hypothesis, as experience shows, may explain all known relevant facts admirably, and yet may at any moment be rendered inadequate by new facts. For this reason, prudent men give only a very provisional assent to a working hypothesis. Thus the cases from which pragmatism endeavours to discover the nature of truth are the very cases in which we have least assurance that truth is present at all. This is certainly a curious and not very hopeful mode of procedure. It may be said, however, that what leads us to feel doubtful about a working hypothesis is merely that it has not yet been shown to work over a sufficiently wide field; the more it works, the more we believe in it. But to this again it may be rejoined that the more it works the less probability is there that any other hypothesis would also work. To pursue this topic, however, would require a discussion of the laws of probability, for which this is not the place.

From what has been said it results that the utmost that pragmatism can derive from science is that the scientific conception of working is not incompatible with the pragmatist conception, since the scientific working may be regarded as a species of the pragmatic working. It is, however, a species whose *differentia* adds just those elements which other philosophies declare to be necessary to truth, while pragmatism declares them to be unnecessary. The essential novelty of pragmatism is that it admits, as a ground of belief, *any kind* of satisfaction to be derived from entertaining the belief, not merely the theoretic satisfaction which is sought by science. For this contention no support whatever is to be found in science. Let us see whether any support is to be found elsewhere.

Pragmatists are never weary of inveighing against those who say that our beliefs *ought* not to be influenced by considerations which in fact do influence them. They point triumphantly to the influence of desire upon belief, and boast that their theory alone is based upon a true psychological account of how belief arises. With this account we have no quarrel; what we deny is its relevance to the question: What is meant by 'truth' and 'falsehood'? At first sight it might seem a perfectly proper inductive proceeding to inquire what properties a belief must have in order that we may call it *true*, and to infer that those properties constitute the meaning of 'truth'. There is, however, a fallacy in this method of inquiry; and this fallacy, in our opinion, is at the bottom of the whole pragmatist philosophy.

There is, in the first place, an ambiguity in the word 'meaning'. We may say 'that cloud means rain', or we may say '*pluie* means rain'. It is obvious that these two senses of 'meaning' are wholly different. What they have in common is that in each case we have one thing which points to another. The cloud is a sign that rain is coming; the word *pluie* is a sign which signifies rain. But beyond this, the two senses of 'meaning' have little in common. In the first sense, one thing 'means' another when the existence (past, present, or future) of the other can be inferred from the one, i.e. when there is a causal connection between them. In the second sense 'meaning' is confined to symbols, i.e. to words, and whatever other ways may be employed for communicating our thoughts. It is this second sense of 'meaning' which we expect a dictionary to give us. When we ask 'What does such and such a word mean?' what we want to know is 'What is in the mind of a person using the word?' A confusion of the two senses of 'meaning' is not uncommon in philosophy; and, if we are not mistaken, pragmatism has confused them in its inquiry as to the 'meaning' of truth. It has discovered something which has a causal connection with our beliefs that things are true, and which, therefore, in the first sense of 'meaning', may be taken to be what these beliefs 'mean'. It has then supposed that this is what is 'meant', in the second sense, by 'truth', i.e. what we have in mind (or should have in mind?) when we use the word 'truth'.

This confusion between the two senses of 'meaning' seems to be necessarily involved in the method adopted by pragmatists, namely, the method which inquires into the causes of our judging things to be true, in the hope of thereby discovering what 'truth' means. Let us grant to the pragmatists, in order to avoid disputes concerning what is unimportant, that what causes people to judge that a belief, about which a doubt has arisen, is true is the fact that this belief is found to further the purposes which led us to inquire into its truth. Then to judge that a belief is true 'means' that this belief furthers our purposes, in the sense in which the cloud 'means' rain, i.e. there is a causal connection between them. But truth is not the same thing as furthering our purposes any more than the cloud is the same thing as rain. When we say that a belief is true, the thought we wish to convey is not the same thought as when we say that the belief furthers our purposes; thus 'true' does not mean 'furthering our purposes' in the sense in which '*pluie*' means rain. Thus pragmatism does not answer the question: What is in our minds when we judge that a certain belief is true?

We find pragmatists, when pressed, willing to admit this fact. Thus Dr Schiller says:[1]

In a sense, therefore, the predications of 'good' and 'bad', 'true' and 'false', etc., may take rank with the experiences of 'sweet', 'red', 'loud', 'hard', etc., as ultimate facts which need be analysed no further.

To which he adds, in a footnote:

The purport of this remark is to confute the notion, which seems dimly to underlie some intellectualist criticisms, that the specific character of the truth-predication is ignored in pragmatist quarters.

This fundamental meaning of 'truth' is treated by Dr Schiller as unimportant because it does not enable us to distinguish the cases in which we have rightly predicted truth from those in which we have done so wrongly. The pragmatist test, he maintains, enables us to distinguish the *truly* true from the *falsely* true. An untested predication of truth

[1] *Studies in Humanism*, p. 144.

he calls 'truth as claim'; a predication which is subsequent
to the application of the pragmatist test he calls 'truth
validated'. The distinction between the two is treated at
length in his essay on 'the ambiguity of truth'.[1] This
'ambiguity' appears to us to be wholly non-existent. The distinction involved is the distinction between what *is* true and
what is *thought to be* true. The reader who will, throughout
this essay on the ambiguity of truth, substitute 'butter' for
'truth' and 'margarine' for 'falsehood', will find that the
point involved is one which has no special relevance to the
nature of truth. There is 'butter as claim', i.e. whatever the
grocer calls butter; this, we will suppose, includes margarine.
There is 'butter validated', which is butter that, after the
usual tests, has been found not to be margarine. But there is
no ambiguity in the word 'butter'. When the grocer, pointing to the margarine, says 'this is butter', he means by 'butter'
precisely what the customer means when he says 'this is not
butter'. To argue from the grocer's language that 'butter' has
two meanings, one of which includes margarine, while the
other does not, would be obviously absurd. Similarly when
the rash man, without applying any tests, affirms 'this belief
is true', while the prudent man, after applying suitable tests,
judges 'this belief is not true', the two men mean the same
thing by the word 'true', only one of them applies it wrongly.
Thus Dr Schiller's reasons for regarding 'the specific character of the truth-predication' as unimportant are not valid.

We must now return to the two senses of 'meaning', and
show how they are relevant to our problem. It is evident that,
in the sense in which the meaning of a word is 'what is in our
minds when we use the word', the meaning of the word
'truth' is just that 'specific character of the truth-predication'
which, as Dr Schiller confesses, is something quite other than
'furthering our purposes'. His contention is that the beliefs of
which we can predicate truth *truly* are those which further
our purposes. And his reason for saying this is that the beliefs
which further our purposes are those which we persist in

[1] *Studies in Humanism*, pp. 141–162.

calling true after reflection. But that only proves that these are the beliefs which we continue to *think* true, not that these are the beliefs which *are* true. Owing, however, to confusion of the two senses of 'meaning', he is led to argue that usefulness gives the *meaning* of truth, and that therefore when a belief is useful it must be true. All that really follows, if we grant the whole of the psychological argument, is that beliefs which are found to be useful will continue to be *thought* to be true. This is an entirely different proposition, and one which, by itself, throws no light whatever either upon the nature of truth or upon what beliefs are in fact true. It may well be that beliefs which fulfil certain purposes are true, while beliefs which fulfil others are not true; or, again, that there is no connection whatever between truth and usefulness. Dr Schiller's argument (and William James's, for the two are practically identical on this point) involves a variety of the very assumption which he criticizes in others, namely, the assumption that all our beliefs are true. In pragmatism the assumption is that the beliefs which we *persist* in holding must be true. It is then pointed out how very unreasonable our grounds often are for persisting in a belief, and this fact, instead of being used to throw doubt on the belief, is used to discredit reasonableness. Thus we are brought back to the standpoint of 'The Will to Believe', and we find that the precepts of that essay really underlie the whole pragmatist theory of truth. But the superstructure is so vast that pragmatists appear to be no longer aware of the foundations upon which their edifice is reared.

We may now restate the pragmatist theory of truth in bald outline, giving due prominence to presuppositions of which pragmatists themselves are perhaps not fully conscious. Their major premiss is: Beliefs which persist after a doubt has been raised are true. Their minor premiss is: Beliefs which are found to be serviceable persist after a doubt has been raised. Hence it follows that such beliefs are true. The pragmatist then turns round and exhorts us to cherish such beliefs, on the ground that they are true. But if his psychology was right the exhortation is needless, since, by his minor premiss, we certainly shall cherish such beliefs. His major premiss should be: 'Beliefs which *we* cherish after *you* have raised a doubt are true.' But those who have raised the doubt can hardly be expected to be much impressed by this premiss. The argument is a form of the old refutation of an opponent by the contention that the whole human race thinks as you do, which is a somewhat unsuccessful weapon against a human being who does not think as you do.

It is now time to turn our attention to the metaphysic which Dr Schiller has based upon the pragmatist theory of truth. Pragmatism as such professes to be only a method; the metaphysical doctrine which Dr Schiller derives from it he calls *Humanism*. In regard to metaphysics, pragmatism professes to be a kind of universal provider, willing and able to suit all tastes. As William James puts it:

Against rationalism as a pretension and a method pragmatism is fully armed and militant. But, at the outset, at least, it stands for no particular results. It has no dogmas, and no doctrines save its method. As the young Italian pragmatist Papini has well said, it lies in the midst of our theories, like a corridor in a hotel. Innumerable chambers open out of it. In one you may find a man writing an atheistic volume; in the next someone on his knees praying for faith and strength; in a third a chemist investigating a body's properties. In a fourth a system of idealistic metaphysics is being excogitated; in a fifth the impossibility of metaphysics is being shown. But they all own the corridor, and all must pass through it if they want a practicable way of getting into or out of their respective rooms.[1]

In spite of this catholicity, however, we agree with Dr Schiller in thinking that his metaphysic is the one which naturally results from pragmatism. It will be remembered that, in considering induction, we pointed to the dependence of inductive verification upon an appeal to 'facts'. Human-

[1] *Pragmatism*, p. 54.

ism, as a metaphysic, results from the application of the pragmatic method to the question: What is a 'fact'? This subject has been treated by Dr Schiller in his essay on 'the making of reality'.[1]

The main purpose of humanist metaphysics is to emphasize the primacy of the Will. The Will, it is true, requires a datum of 'fact' to which to apply its operations, but this datum is itself the product of previous volitions, and although we cannot quite deny some original ὕλη which has been moulded by will, yet this is remote and unimportant, and has been transformed into genuine reality by the agency of human beings and other beings more or less resembling them. Nothing that can be known, nothing that can properly be called 'real', is independent of the knower. There is no such thing as 'mere' knowing, in which we passively apprehend the nature of a merely 'given' object. All knowing is bound up with doing and everything that we know has been in some degree altered by our agency. This, Dr Schiller says, is óbvious in the case of our acquaintances, who plainly are more or less affected by the fact that we are acquainted with them. When we say that something is 'independent' of our knowing, we mean, according to him, that the thing is not aware that we know it. But, as a matter of fact, everything we know, even a stone, is aware of us in its own way. To the charge that this is Hylozoism, Dr Schiller replies by admitting it.

The grounds for these opinions are not set forth quite so clearly as could be wished, but we may gather them from a complimentary allusion to Hegel's dialectic at the beginning of the essay. Imagine some 'fact' in regard to which we entertain a belief. The belief leads to action, and the action alters the 'fact'. If it alters it into harmony with our wishes the belief is proved to have been what pragmatists call 'true', since it has proved successful in action. In this case, since the belief in the fact is true, it follows that the fact is real. Thus the belief has made the fact. But if the outcome of the belief is a 'fact' which, though in harmony with the wishes which

[1] *Studies in Humanism*, pp. 421–51.

originally led us to concern ourselves with the matter, is in conflict with others of our wishes, the belief is not 'true' as regards these other wishes; hence we shall have to change our belief, and take fresh action on the new belief, and so bring the 'fact' into harmony with these new wishes. In this way, so long as we have any unsatisfied wishes, we are led on in a cycle of beliefs and actions, the beliefs becoming gradually 'truer', and the 'facts' with which the beliefs are concerned becoming gradually more 'real' as greater harmony is established between the 'facts' and our wishes. The motive power of this whole development is the pragmatic definition of truth. For if we believe A to be a fact, that belief is true if it is successful as a means to satisfying our wishes; hence so long as our wishes are not completely satisfied, the belief that A is a fact is not completely true, and therefore A is not completely a fact. Thus complete truth and complete reality go hand in hand, and both are only to be found at the end of the road which leads to the complete satisfaction of all our wishes.

The similarity of the above process to the Hegelian dialectic is emphasized by Dr Schiller: with his inveterate love of a pun, he has christened his process 'trialectic'. He does not seem, however, to have observed that his process, like Hegel's, introduces a distinction between appearance and reality; that appearance embraces the whole of the world as we know it, and that it is only to reality that the pragmatic test of truth applies. The 'facts' which he can accept as real must be such as not to thwart our purposes; the 'facts' which appear are very often such as to thwart our purposes. If a fact is such as to thwart our purposes, the pragmatist test of truth is not fully applicable to it; for by believing that it will thwart our purposes, we do not prevent it from doing so, and our belief, though possibly preferable pragmatically to any other, does not secure the satisfaction of our desires. If, on the other hand, we believe that the fact is *not* such as to thwart our purposes, we believe what, *ex hypothesi*, is not the case. Hence it follows that such facts cannot be real. Since many apparent facts thwart our purposes, we are led to distinguish between real and apparent facts. Hence it is not here on earth that pragmatism applies, but only in Dr Schiller's heaven, just as it is only in Mr Bradley's heaven that Mr Bradley's metaphysic applies. The whole doctrine, therefore, reduces itself to the proposition that it would be heavenly to live in a world where one's philosophy was true, and this is a proposition which we have no desire to controvert.

The distinction between appearance and reality is one which Dr Schiller is never weary of attacking; indeed, a very large proportion of his writings is directed against it. His complete reality, he holds, is being progressively realized, and is not, like the Absolute, something wholly unconnected with our actual world of appearance. But his only reason for supposing that his complete reality is being progressively realized is a tacit assumption of co-operation among the agents composing the universe. He assumes, that is, that the various desires which (according to him) form the motive power of all that occurs in the universe are not such as to countract each other: the world's activities are not to be conceived as a tug-of-war. For this view there is, we fancy, no argument except the pragmatic argument, that it is pleasant and cannot be conclusively disproved.

Thus the whole humanist metaphysic rests upon the pragmatic theory of truth, and falls with that theory. Moreover, it introduces, in a slightly modified form, the old distinction of appearance and reality, of which the difficulties have been admirably set forth by Dr Schiller himself. Since the distinction, and therefore the difficulties, result inevitably from the pragmatic theory of truth, they afford a new argument against that theory; for they show that the theory is applicable, not to our actual world, but to an ideal world where all the hopes of pragmatists have been realized.

Although, for the reasons alleged above, we do not ourselves accept the pragmatist philosophy, we nevertheless believe that it is likely to achieve widespread popularity, because it embodies some of the main intellectual and political tendencies of our time. This aspect of pragmatism deserves consideration, since the influence of a doctrine (as pragmatists have very prudently pointed out) is by no means proportional to its intellectual value.

On the intellectual side, pragmatism embodies scepticism, evolution, and the new insight into the nature and scope of scientific induction. On the political side, it embodies democracy, the increased belief in human power which has come from the progress of mechanical invention, and the Bismarckian belief in force.

The scepticism embodied in pragmatism is that which says, 'Since all beliefs are absurd, we may as well believe what is most convenient.' This is by no means a new contention; in England it has been popularized by Mr Balfour's *Foundations of Belief* and *Notes on Insular Free Trade*. Scepticism is of the very essence of the pragmatic philosophy: nothing is certain, everything is liable to revision, and the attainment of any truth in which we can rest securely is impossible. It is, therefore, not worth while to trouble our heads about what really is true; what is *thought* to be true is all that need concern us. Instead of the old distinction between 'true' and 'false', we adopt the more useful distinction between what we persist in thinking true, and what merely seems true at first sight. Later on, the old meanings of 'true' and 'false' may slip back unnoticed, and we may come to think that what is true in the pragmatic sense is true in the old sense also; this happens especially in regard to religion. But on pragmatist principles, there is no reason to regret this; for the 'true' is what it is useful to believe, and therefore it is useful to believe what pragmatism declares to be true. Scepticism, therefore, though necessary at the start, must be banished later on if we are to get the full benefits of pragmatism. In this there is no great psychological difficulty, since, as Hume confessed, the sceptical attitude is one not easily maintained in practice.

The philosophy of evolution has also had its share in generating the pragmatic tone of mind. It has led people to regard everything as fluid and in process of development, everything as passing by imperceptible gradations into everything else. Some biologists, it is true, have begun to regard development as discontinuous, proceeding by the sudden appearance of freaks; but philosophers and the general public have not been influenced by this change. Hence it has come to be felt that all sharp antitheses, such as that of *true* and *false*, must be blurred, and all finality must be avoided. We must always build a road by which everything can pass into everything else at a leisurely pace and with small steps. Instead of 'the true' we shall have 'the more true', or 'the most true up to date'. And between different claimants for truth, we must provide a struggle for existence, leading to the survival of the strongest. All this is admirably effected by the pragmatic theory of truth. M. Bergson, whom pragmatists claim as an ally, may be regarded as embodying this tendency.

The influence of modern theories of scientific induction has probably been more restricted, in point of numbers, than the influence of scepticism or of evolution, but the men influenced have been important by their scientific eminence. We may take as their protagonist M. Poincaré, who, while not extending the pragmatist doctrine to particular facts, has dealt in a thoroughly pragmatic spirit with the general hypotheses of logic, mathematics, and physics, showing that what leads to the acceptance of a scientific hypothesis is its *convenience*. Such general assumptions as causality, the existence of an external world, etc., cannot be supported by Mill's canons of induction, but require a far more comprehensive treatment of the whole organized body of accepted scientific doctrine. It is in such treatment that the pragmatic method is seen at its best; and among men of science its apparent success in this direction has doubtless contributed greatly to its acceptance.

The influence of democracy in promoting pragmatism is visible in almost every page of William James's writing. There is an impatience of authority, an unwillingness to condemn widespread prejudices, a tendency to decide philosophical questions by putting them to the vote, which contrast curiously with the usual dictatorial tone of philosophic writings. Dr Schiller at one time set to work to elucidate the question of a future life by taking a poll.[1] William James claims for the pragmatist temper 'the open air and possibilities of nature, as against dogma, artificiality, and the pretence of finality in truth'. A thing which simply *is* true, whether you like it or not, is to him as hateful as a Russian autocracy; he feels that he is escaping from a prison, made not by stone walls but by 'hard facts', when he has humanized truth, and made it, like the police force in a democracy, the servant of the people instead of their master. The democratic temper pervades even the religion of the pragmatists: they have the religion they have chosen, and the traditional reverence is changed into satisfaction with their own handiwork. 'The prince of darkness', James says, 'may be a gentleman, as we are told he is, but whatever the God of earth and heaven is, he can surely be no gentleman.'[2] He is rather, we should say, conceived by pragmatists as an elected president, to whom we give a respect which is really a tribute to the wisdom of our own choice. A government in which we have no voice is repugnant to the democratic temper. William James carries up to heaven the revolt of his New England ancestors: the Power to which he can yield respect must be a George Washington rather than a George III.

Closely connected with this democratic spirit is the belief in human power, which is one of the dominant notes of pragmatism. By the progress of mechanical invention, the possibilities of our command over nature have been shown to be much greater than they were formerly supposed to be, and no definite limits can be set to them. Hence has arisen—especially in America, where the economic conditions are favourable, and the chief concern of most people is with those matters in which recent advances have been greatest—a

[1] See his essay on 'The Desire for Immortality' (*Humanism*, pp. 228–49). We do not, of course, suggest that he would have considered the result of the poll decisive, even if the electorate had been larger.

[2] *Pragmatism*, p. 72.

general feeling that by energy and hope all obstacles can be overcome, and that it is a mark of laziness or pusillanimity to admit that anything is impossible. The habit of mind which believes that there are no essential impossibilities has been fostered by the doctrine of evolution, with its literary corollary of the *Uebermensch*. Hence have arisen a self-confidence and a pride of life which in many ways remind one of the Renaissance, and establish some affinity between historical humanism and its modern namesake. For the modern humanism is essentially the philosophy which is appropriate, as Dr Schiller himself has said, to 'the young, the strong, the virile'.[1] The inventor, the financier, the advertiser, the successful men of action generally, can find in pragmatism an expression of their instinctive view of the world. Such men, both for good and evil, expect the world to be malleable to their wishes, and in a greater or less degree find their expectation justified by success. Hence arises a disbelief in those 'hard facts' which pragmatists tend to deny, and a confidence of victory in contests with the outer world, whether these contests be cognitive or more directly practical. An Italian pragmatist has expressed this confidence in victory as follows:

> Dio è perfetto perchè è onnipossente. Sostituiamo dunque al misticismo della rinunzia, dell' *Imitazione di Cristo*, il misticismo della conquista, dell' *Imitazione di Dio*.[2]

Other pragmatists have been less explicit than this modern Thomas à Kempis, but he has correctly expressed the spirit of their philosophy.

From the confidence of victory in contests it is an easy passage to the love of contest. For this pragmatism provides full scope. The many different 'truths as claim' must fight it out among themselves. and the victor will become 'truth validated'. Dr Schiller on one occasion implicitly confesses that, with his theory of truth, persecution can actually make a doctrine true which would otherwise be false, since it can

[1] *Humanism*, p. viii.
[2] Leonardo, April 1905, *L'Imitazione d' Iddio*, p. 64.

make a doctrine 'useful to our lives'.[1] In the absence of any standard of truth other than success, it seems evident that the familiar methods of the struggle for existence must be applied to the elucidation of difficult questions, and that ironclads and Maxim guns must be the ultimate arbiters of meta-physical truth.

The worship of force, as we find it in Nietzsche, is not to be found in the same form in William James, who, though he lauds the will and the life of action, does not wish action to be bellicose. Nevertheless, the excessive individualism of the pragmatic theory of truth is inherently connected with the appeal to force. If there is a non-human truth, which one man may know, while another does not, there is a standard outside the disputants, to which, we may urge, the dispute ought to be submitted; hence a pacific and judicial settle-ment of disputes is at least theoretically possible. If, on the contrary, the only way of discovering which of the disputants is in the right is to wait and see which of them is successful, there is no longer any principle except force by which the issue can be decided. It is true, of course, that in a private dispute the public opinion of the community, especially as embodied in the law, will usually compel a peaceful decision. But this public opinion is formed (at least in theory) upon an objective estimate of the rights and wrongs of the case; in place of this, if pragmatism were the accepted creed, public opinion would have to be guided by the interests of the com-munity. To this there would be no objection if, as would commonly be done, the maintenance of justice could be taken as one of the ends which it is in the interest of the com-munity to pursue. But in a pragmatist community this would be impossible, since justice is derivative from the interests of the community, and not an independent constituent of those interests. In international matters, owing to the fact that the disputants are often strong enough to be independent of out-

[1] *Humanism*, p. 59: 'Delicate questions may arise out of the fact that not only does what works receive social recognition, but also that what receives social recognition for this very reason largely works.'

side control, these considerations become more important. If the pragmatist urges that always and everywhere the only ultimate arbiter in a dispute *must* be force, the reply is that, although this is true, at the actual moment of the battle, it is yet not true in a wider sense, since it ignores the motives which generate the force on either side. The hopes of international peace, like the achievement of internal peace, depend upon the creation of an effective force of public opinion formed upon an estimate of the rights and wrongs of disputes. Thus it would be misleading to say that the dispute is decided by force, without adding that force is dependent upon justice. But the possibility of such a public opinion depends upon the possibility of a standard of justice which is a cause, not an effect, of the wishes of the community; and such a standard of justice seems incompatible with the pragmatist philosophy. This philosophy, therefore, although it begins with liberty and toleration, develops, by inherent necessity, into the appeal to force and the arbitrament of the big battalions. By this development it becomes equally adapted to democracy at home and to imperialism abroad. Thus here, again, it is more delicately adjusted to the requirements of the time than any other philosophy which has hitherto been invented.

To sum up: Pragmatism appeals to the temper of mind which finds on the surface of this planet the whole of its imaginative material; which feels confident of progress, and unaware of non-human limitations to human power; which loves battle, with all the attendant risks, because it has no real doubt that it will achieve victory; which desires religion, as it desires railways and electric light, as a comfort and a help in the affairs of this world, not as providing non-human objects to satisfy the hunger for perfection and for something to be worshipped without reserve. But for those who feel that life on this planet would be a life in prison if it were not for the windows into a greater world beyond; for those to whom a belief in man's omnipotence seems arrogant, who desire rather the Stoic freedom that comes of mastery over the passions than the Napoleonic domination that sees the kingdoms of this world at its feet—in a word, to men who do not find Man an adequate object of their worship, the pragmatist's world will seem narrow and petty, robbing life of all that gives it value, and making Man himself smaller by depriving the universe which he contemplates of all its splendour.

V

WILLIAM JAMES'S CONCEPTION
OF TRUTH[1]

'The history of philosophy', as William James observes, 'is to a great extent that of a certain clash of human temperaments.' In dealing with a temperament of such charm as his, it is not pleasant to think of a 'clash'; one does not willingly differ, or meet so much urbanity by churlish criticisms. Fortunately, a very large part of his book is concerned with the advocacy of positions which pragmatism shares with other forms of empiricism; with all this part of his book, I, as an empiricist, find myself, broadly speaking, in agreement. I might instance the lecture devoted to a problem which he considers 'the most central of all philosophic problems', namely, that of the One and the Many. In this lecture he declares himself on the whole a pluralist, after a discussion of the kinds and degrees of unity to be found in the world to which any empiricist may wholly assent. Throughout the book, the distinctive tenets of pragmatism only ·make their appearance now and again, after the ground has been carefully prepared. James speaks somewhere of Dr Schiller's 'butt-end foremost statement of the humanist position'. His own statement is the very reverse of 'butt-end foremost'; it is insinuating, gradual, imperceptible.

A good illustration of his insinuating method is afforded by

[1] *Pragmatism: a new name for some old ways of thinking.* Popular Lectures on Philosophy, by William James (Longmans, Green, and Co., 1907). The following article is reprinted from the *Albany Review*, January 1908, where it appeared under the title 'Transatlantic "Truth"'. It has been criticized by William James in *The Meaning of Truth* (Longmans, 1909), in the article called 'Two English Critics'.

his lecture on common sense. The categories of common sense, as he points out, and as we may all agree, embody discoveries of our remote ancestors; but these discoveries cannot be regarded as final, because science, and still more philosophy, finds common-sense notions inadequate in many ways. Common sense, science, and philosophy, we are told, are all insufficiently true in some respect; and to this again we may agree. But he adds: 'It is evident that the conflict of these so widely differing systems obliges us to overhaul the very idea of truth, for at present we have no definite notion of what the word may mean' (p. 192). Here, as I think, we have a mere *non sequitur*. A damson-tart, a plum-tart, and a gooseberry-tart may all be insufficiently sweet; but does that oblige us to overhaul the very notion of sweetness, or show that we have no definite notion of what the word 'sweetness' may mean? It seems to me, on the contrary, that if we perceive that they are insufficiently sweet, that shows that we do know what 'sweetness' is; and the same surely applies to truth. But this remark is merely by the way.

James, like most philosophers, represents his views as mediating between two opposing schools. He begins by distinguishing two philosophic types called respectively the 'tender-minded' and the 'tough-minded'. The 'tender-minded' are 'rationalistic, intellectualistic, idealistic, optimistic, religious, free-willist, monistic, dogmatical'. The 'tough-minded' are 'empiricist, sensationalistic, materialistic, pessimistic, irreligious, fatalistic, pluralistic, sceptical'. Traditionally, German philosophy was on the whole 'tender-minded', British philosophy was on the whole 'tough-minded'. It will clear the ground for me to confess at once that I belong, with some reserves, to the 'tough-minded' type. Pragmatism, William James avers, 'can satisfy both kinds of demand. It can remain religious like the rationalisms, but at the same time, like the empiricisms, it can preserve the richest intimacy with facts'. This reconciliation, to my mind, is illusory; I find myself agreeing with the 'tough-minded' half of pragmatism and totally disagreeing with the 'tender-minded' half. But the disentagling of the two halves must be postponed till we have seen how the reconciliation professes to be effected. Pragmatism represents, on the one hand, a method and habit of mind, on the other, a certain theory as to what constitutes truth. The latter is more nearly what Dr Schiller calls humanism; but this name is not adopted by James. We must, therefore, distinguish the pragmatic *method* and the pragmatic *theory of truth*. The former, up to a point, is involved in all induction, and is certainly largely commendable. The latter is the essential novelty and the point of real importance. But let us first consider the pragmatic method.

'Pragmatism', says James, 'represents a perfectly familiar attitude in philosophy, the empiricist attitude, but it represents it, as it seems to me, both in a more radical and in a less objectionable form than it has ever yet assumed. A pragmatist turns his back resolutely and once for all upon a lot of inveterate habits dear to professional philosophers. He turns away from abstraction and insufficiency, from verbal solutions, from bad *a priori* reasons, from fixed principles, closed systems, and pretended absolutes and origins. He turns towards concreteness and adequacy towards facts, towards action and towards power. That means the empiricist temper regnant and the rationalist temper sincerely given up. It means the open air and possibilities of nature, as against dogma, artificiality, and the pretence of finality in truth' (p. 51).

The temper of mind here described is one with which I, for my part, in the main cordially sympathize. But I think there is an impression in the mind of William James, as of some other pragmatists, that pragmatism involves a more open mind than its opposite. As regards scientific questions, or even the less important questions of philosophy, this is no doubt more or less the case. But as regards the fundamental questions of philosophy—especially as regards what I consider *the* fundamental question, namely, the nature of truth— pragmatism is absolutely dogmatic. The hypothesis that

pragmatism is erroneous is not allowed to enter for the pragmatic competition; however well it may work, it is not to be
entertained. To 'turn your back resolutely and once for all'
upon the philosophy of others may be heroic or praiseworthy,
but it is not undogmatic or open-minded. A modest shrinking
from self-assertion, a sense that all our theories are provisional, a constant realization that after all the hypothesis of
our opponents may be the right one—these characterize the
truly empirical temper, but I do not observe that they invari-
ably characterize the writings of pragmatists. Dogmatism in
fundamentals is more or less unavoidable in philosophy, and
I do not blame pragmatists for what could not be otherwise;
but I demur to their claim to a greater open-mindedness than
is or may be possessed by their critics.

William James, however, it must be admitted, is about as
little pontifical as a philosopher well can be. And his complete absence of unction is most refreshing. 'In this real world
of sweat and dirt', he says, 'it seems to me that when a view
of things is "noble", that ought to count as a presumption
against its truth and as a philosophic disqualification' (p. 72).
Accordingly his contentions are never supported by 'fine
writing'; he brings them into the market-place, and is not
afraid to be homely, untechnical, and slangy. All this makes
his books refreshing to read, and shows that they contain
what he really lives by, not merely what he holds in his professional capacity.

But it is time to return to the pragmatic method.

'The pragmatic method', we are told, 'is primarily a
method of settling metaphysical disputes that otherwise
might be interminable. Is the world one or many?—fated
or free?—material or spiritual?—here are notions either of
which may or may not hold good of the world; and disputes
over such notions are unending. The pragmatic method in
such cases is to try to interpret each notion by tracing its respective practical consequences. What difference would it
practically make to anyone if this notion rather than that
notion were true? If no practical difference whatever can be

traced, then the alternatives mean practically the same thing, and all dispute is idle. Whenever a dispute is serious, we ought to be able to show some practical difference that must follow from one side or the other's being right.' And again: 'To attain perfect clearness in our thoughts of an object, then, we need only consider what conceivable effects of a practical kind the object may involve—what sensations we are to expect from it, and what reactions we must prepare. Our conception of these effects, whether immediate or remote, is then for us the whole of our conception of the object, so far as that conception has positive significance at all' (pp. 45–7).

To this method, applied within limits and to suitable topics, there is no ground for objecting. On the contrary, it is wholesome to keep in touch with concrete facts, as far as possible, by remembering to bring our theories constantly into connection with them. The method, however, involves more than is stated in the extract which I quoted just now. It involves also the suggestion of the pragmatic criterion of truth: a belief is to be judged true in so far as the practical consequences of its adoption are good. Some pragmatists, for example, Le Roy (who has lately suffered Papal condemnation), regard the pragmatic test as giving *only* a criterion;[1] others, notably Dr Schiller, regard it as giving the actual *meaning* of truth. William James agrees on this point with Dr Schiller, though, like him, he does not enter into the question of criterion *versus* meaning.

The pragmatic theory of truth is the central doctrine of pragmatism, and we must consider it at some length. William James states it in various ways, some of which I shall now quote. He says: 'Ideas (which themselves are but parts of our experience) become true just in so far as they help us to get into satisfactory relation with other parts of our experience' (p. 58). Again: 'Truth is *one species of good*, and not, as is usually supposed, a category distinct from good, and co-ordinate with it. *The true is the name of whatever proves itself to be*

[1] Cf., e.g., Le Roy, 'Comment se pose le problème de Dieu', *Revue de Métaphysique et de Morale*, xv 4 (July 1907), pp. 506, 507 *n*.

good in the way of belief, and good, too, for definite, assignable reasons' (p. 75). That truth means 'agreement with reality' may be said by a pragmatist as well as by anyone else, but the pragmatist differs from others as to what is meant by 'agreement', and also (it would seem) as to what is meant by 'reality'. William James gives the following definition of 'agreement': 'To "agree" in the widest sense with a reality *can only mean to be guided either straight up to it or into its surroundings, or to be put into such working touch with it as to handle either it or something connected with it better than if we disagreed*' (p. 212). This language is rather metaphorical, and a little puzzling; it is plain, however, that 'agreement' is regarded as practical, not as merely intellectual. This emphasis on practice is, of course, one of the leading features of pragmatism.

In order to understand the pragmatic notion of truth, we have to be clear as to the basis of *fact* upon which truths are supposed to rest. Immediate sensible experience, for example, does not come under the alternative of *true* and *false*. 'Day follows day', says James, 'and its contents are simply added. The new contents themselves are not true, they simply *come* and *are*. Truth is *what we say about* them' (p. 62). Thus when we are merely aware of sensible objects, we are not to be regarded as knowing any truth, although we have a certain kind of contact with reality. It is important to realize that the *facts* which thus lie outside the scope of truth and falsehood supply the material which is presupposed by the pragmatic theory. Our beliefs have to agree with matters of fact: it is an essential part of their 'satisfactoriness' that they should do so. James also mentions what he calls 'relations among purely mental ideas' as part of our stock-in-trade with which pragmatism starts. He mentions as instances '1 and 1 make 2', 'white differs less from grey than it does from black', and so on. All such propositions as these, then, we are supposed to know for certain before we can get under way. As James puts it: 'Between the coercions of the sensible order and those of the ideal order, our mind is thus wedged tightly. Our ideas must agree with realities, be such realities concrete or abstract, be they facts or be they principles, under penalty of endless inconsistency and frustration' (p. 211). Thus it is only when we pass beyond plain matters of fact and *a priori* truisms that the pragmatic notion of truth comes in. It is, in short, the notion to be applied to doubtful cases, but it is not the notion to be applied to cases about which there can be no doubt. And that there are cases about which there can be no doubt is presupposed in the very statement of the pragmatist position. 'Our account of truth', James tells us, 'is an account . . . of processes of leading, realized *in rebus*, and having only this quality in common, that they *pay*' (p. 218). We may thus sum up the philosophy in the following definition: 'A truth is anything which it pays to believe.' Now, if this definition is to be useful, as pragmatism intends it to be, it must be possible to know that it pays to believe something without knowing anything that pragmatism would call a truth. Hence the knowledge that a certain belief pays must be classed as knowledge of a sensible fact or of a 'relation among purely mental ideas', or as some compound of the two, and must be so easy to discover as not to be worthy of having the pragmatic test applied to it. There is, however, some difficulty in this view. Let us consider for a moment what it means to say that a belief 'pays'. We must suppose that this means that the consequences of entertaining the belief are better than those of rejecting it. In order to know this, we must know what are the consequences of entertaining it, and what are the consequences of rejecting it; we must know also what consequences are good, what bad, what consequences are better, and what worse. Take, say, belief in the Roman Catholic Faith. This, we may agree, causes a certain amount of happiness at the expense of a certain amount of stupidity and priestly domination. Such a view is disputable and disputed, but we will let that pass. But then comes the question whether, admitting the effects to be such, they are to be classed as on the whole good or on the whole bad; and this question is one which is so difficult that our test of truth becomes practically useless. It is far easier, it seems to me, to settle the plain question of fact: 'Have Popes been always infallible?' than to settle the question whether the effects of thinking them infallible are on the whole good. Yet this question, of the truth of Roman Catholicism, is just the sort of question that pragmatists consider specially suitable to their method.

The notion that it is quite easy to know when the consequences of a belief are good, so easy, in fact, that a theory of knowledge need take no account of anything so simple—this notion, I must say, seems to me one of the strangest assumptions for a theory of knowledge to make. Let us take another illustration. Many of the men of the French Revolution were disciples of Rousseau, and their belief in his doctrines had far-reaching effects, which make Europe at this day a different place from what it would have been without that belief. If, on the whole, the effects of their belief have been good, we shall have to say that their belief was true; if bad, that it was false. But how are we to strike the balance? It is almost impossible to disentangle what the effects have been; and even if we could ascertain them, our judgment as to whether they have been good or bad would depend upon our political opinions. It is surely far easier to discover by direct investigation that the *Contrat Social* is a myth than to decide whether belief in it has done harm or good on the whole.

Another difficulty which I feel in regard to the pragmatic meaning of 'truth' may be stated as follows: Suppose I accept the pragmatic criterion, and suppose you persuade me that a certain belief is useful. Suppose I thereupon conclude that the belief is true. Is it not obvious that there is a transition in my mind from seeing that the belief is useful to actually holding that the belief is true? Yet this could not be so if the pragmatic account of truth were valid. Take, say, the belief that other people exist. According to the pragmatists, to say 'it is true that other people exist' *means* 'it is useful to believe that other people exist'. But if so, then these two phrases are merely different words for the same proposition; therefore when I believe the one I believe the other. If this were so, there could be no transition from the one to the other, as plainly there is. This shows that the word 'true' represents for us a different idea from that represented by the phrase 'useful to believe', and that, therefore, the pragmatic definition of truth ignores, without destroying, the meaning commonly given to the word 'true', which meaning, in my opinion, is of fundamental importance, and can only be ignored at the cost of hopeless inadequacy.

This brings me to the difference between *criterion* and *meaning*—a point on which neither James nor Dr Schiller is very clear. I may best explain the difference, to begin with, by an instance. If you wish to know whether a certain book is in a library, you consult the catalogue: books mentioned in the catalogue are presumably in the library, books not mentioned in it are presumably not in the library. Thus the catalogue affords a *criterion* of whether a book is in the library or not. But even supposing the catalogue perfect, it is obvious that when you say the book is in the library you do not *mean* that it is mentioned in the catalogue. You mean that the actual book is to be found somewhere in the shelves. It therefore remains an intelligible hypothesis that there are books in the library which are not yet catalogued, or that there are books catalogued which have been lost and are no longer in the library. And it remains an inference from the discovery that a book is mentioned in the catalogue to the conclusion that the book is in the library. Speaking abstractly, we may say that a property A is a *criterion* of a property B when the same objects possess both; and A is a *useful* criterion of B if it is easier to discover whether an object possesses the property A than whether it possesses the property B. Thus being mentioned in the catalogue is a *useful* criterion of being in the library, because it is easier to consult the catalogue than to hunt through the shelves.

Now if pragmatists only affirmed that utility is a *criterion* of truth, there would be much less to be said against their view. For there certainly seem to be few cases, if any, in which it is clearly useful to believe what is false. The chief criticism one would then have to make on pragmatism would be to deny that utility is a *useful* criterion, because it is so often harder to determine whether a belief is useful than whether it is true. The arguments of pragmatists are almost wholly directed to proving that utility is a *criterion*; that utility is the *meaning* of truth is then supposed to follow. But, to return to our illustration of the library, suppose we had conceded that there are no mistakes in the British Museum catalogue: would it follow that the catalogue would do without the books? We can imagine some person long engaged in a comparative study of libraries, and having, in the process, naturally lost all taste for reading, declaring that the catalogue is the only important thing—as for the books, they are useless lumber; no one ever wants them, and the principle of economy should lead us to be content with the catalogue. Indeed, if you consider the matter with an open mind, you will see that the catalogue *is* the library, for it tells you everything you can possibly wish to know about the library. Let us, then, save the taxpayers' money by destroying the books: allow free access to the catalogue, but condemn the desire to read as involving an exploded dogmatic realism.

This analogy of the library is not, to my mind, fantastic or unjust, but as close and exact an analogy as I have been able to think of. The point I am trying to make clear is concealed from pragmatists, I think, by the fact that their theories start very often from such things as the general hypotheses of science—ether, atoms, and the like. In such cases, we take little interest in the hypotheses themselves, which, as we well know, are liable to rapid change. What we care about are the inferences as to sensible phenomena which the hypotheses enable us to make. All we ask of the hypotheses is that they should 'work'—though it should be observed that what constitutes 'working' is not the general agreeableness of their results, but the conformity of these results with observed phenomena. But in the case of these general scientific hypotheses, no sensible man believes that they are true as they stand. They are believed to be true in part, and to work because of the part that is true; but it is expected that in time some element of falsehood will be discovered, and some truer theory will be substituted. Thus pragmatism would seem to derive its notion of what constitutes belief from cases in which, properly speaking, belief is absent, and in which—what is pragmatically important—there is but a slender interest in truth or falsehood as compared to the interest in what 'works'.

But when this method is extended to cases in which the proposition in question has an emotional interest on its own account, apart from its working, the pragmatic account becomes less satisfactory. This point has been well brought out by Professor Stout in *Mind*[1], and what I have to say is mostly contained in his remarks. Take the question whether other people exist. It seems perfectly possible to suppose that the hypothesis that they exist will always work, even if they do not in fact exist. It is plain, also, that it makes for happiness to believe that they exist—for even the greatest misanthropist would not wish to be deprived of the objects of his hate. Hence the belief that other people exist is, pragmatically, a true belief. But if I am troubled by solipsism, the discovery that a belief in the existence of others is 'true' in the pragmatist's sense is not enough to allay my sense of loneliness: the perception that I should profit by rejecting solipsism is not alone sufficient to make me reject it. For what I desire is not that the belief in solipsism should be false in the pragmatic sense, but that other people should in fact exist. And with the pragmatist's meaning of truth, these two do not necessarily go together. The belief in solipsism might be false even if I were the only person or thing in the universe.

This paradoxical consequence would, I presume, not be admitted by pragmatists. Yet it is an inevitable outcome of the divorce which they make between *fact* and *truth*. Returning to our illustration, we may say that 'facts' are represented

[1] October 1907, pp. 586–8. This criticism occurs in the course of a very sympathetic review of Dr Schiller's *Studies in Humanism*.

by the books, and 'truths' by the entries in the catalogue. So long as you do not wish to read the books, the 'truths' will do in place of the 'facts', and the imperfections of your library can be remedied by simply making new entries in the catalogue. But as soon as you actually wish to read a book, the 'truths' become inadequate, and the 'facts' become all-important. The pragmatic account of truth assumes, so it seems to me, that no one takes any interest in facts, and that the truth of the proposition that your friend exists is an adequate substitute for the fact of his existence. 'Facts', they tell us, are neither true nor false, therefore truth cannot be concerned with them. But the truth 'A exists', if it is a truth, is concerned with A, who in that case is a fact; and to say that 'A exists' may be true even if A does not exist is to give a meaning to 'truth' which robs it of all interest. Dr Schiller is fond of attacking the view that truth must correspond with reality; we may conciliate him by agreeing that *his* truth, at any rate, need not correspond with reality. But we shall have to add that reality is to us more interesting than such truth.

I am, of course, aware that pragmatists minimize the basis of 'fact', and speak of the 'making of reality' as proceeding *pari passu* with the 'making of truth'. It is easy to criticize the claim to 'make reality' except within obvious limits. But when such criticisms are met by pointing to the pragmatist's admission that, after all, there must be a basis of 'fact' for our creative activity to work upon, then the opposite line of criticism comes into play. Dr Schiller, in his essay on 'the making of reality', minimizes the importance of the basis of 'fact', on the ground (it would seem) that 'facts' will not submit to pragmatic treatment, and that, if pragmatism is true, they are unknowable.[1] Hence, on pragmatistic principles, it is useless to think about facts. We therefore return to fictions with a sigh of relief, and soothe our scruples by calling them 'realities'. But it seems something of a *petitio principii* to condemn 'facts' because pragmatism, though it finds them

[1] Cf. *Studies in Humanism*, pp. 434–6.

necessary, is unable to deal with them. And William James, it should be said, makes less attempt than Dr Schiller does to minimize facts. In this essay, therefore, I have considered the difficulties which pragmatism has to face if it admits 'facts' rather than those (no less serious) which it has to face if it denies them.

It is chiefly in regard to religion that the pragmatist use of 'truth' seems to me misleading. Pragmatists boast much of their ability to reconcile religion and science, and William James, as we saw, professes to have discovered a position combining the merits of tender-mindedness and tough-mindedness. The combination is really effected, if I am not mistaken, in a way of which pragmatists are not themselves thoroughly aware. For their position, if they fully realized it, would, I think, be this: 'We cannot know whether, in fact, there is a God or a future life, but we can know that the belief in God and a future life is true.' This position, it is to be feared, would not afford much comfort to the religious if it were understood, and I cannot but feel some sympathy with the Pope in his condemnation of it.

'On pragmatic principles', James says, 'we cannot reject any hypothesis if consequences useful to life flow from it' (p. 273). He proceeds to point out that consequences useful to life flow from the hypothesis of the Absolute, which is therefore so far a true hypothesis. But it should be observed that these useful consequences flow from the hypothesis that the Absolute is a fact, not from the hypothesis that useful consequences flow from belief in the Absolute. But we cannot believe the hypothesis that the Absolute is a fact merely because we perceive that useful consequences flow from this hypothesis. What we can believe on such grounds is that this hypothesis is what pragmatists call 'true', i.e. that it is useful; but it is not from this belief that the useful consequences flow, and the grounds alleged do not make us believe that the Absolute is a fact, which is the useful belief. In other words, the useful belief is that the Absolute is a fact, and pragmatism shows that this belief is what it calls 'true'. Thus pragmatism persuades us that belief in the Absolute is 'true', but does not persuade us that the Absolute is a fact. The belief which it persuades us to adopt is therefore not the one which is useful. In ordinary logic, if the belief in the Absolute is true, it follows that the Absolute is a fact. But with the pragmatist's meaning of 'true' this does not follow; hence the proposition which he proves is not, as he thinks, the one from which comforting consequences flow.

In another place James says: 'On pragmatistic principles, if the hypothesis of God works satisfactorily in the widest sense of the word, it is true' (p. 299). This proposition is, in reality, a mere tautology. For we have laid down the definition: 'The word "true" means "working satisfactorily in the widest sense of the word".' Hence the proposition stated by James is merely a verbal variant on the following: 'On pragmatistic principles, if the hypothesis of God works satisfactorily in the widest sense of the word, then it works satisfactorily in the widest sense of the word.' This would hold even on other than pragmatistic principles; presumably what is peculiar to pragmatism is the belief that this is an important contribution to the philosophy of religion. The advantage of the pragmatic method is that it decides the question of the truth of the existence of God by purely mundane arguments, namely, by the effects of belief in His existence upon our life in this world. But unfortunately this gives a merely mundane conclusion, namely, that belief in God is true, i.e. useful, whereas what religion desires is the conclusion that God exists, which pragmatism never even approaches. I infer, therefore, that the pragmatic philosophy of religion, like most philosophies whose conclusions are interesting, turns on an unconscious play upon words. A common word—in this case, the word 'true'—is taken at the outset in an uncommon sense, but as the argument proceeds, the usual sense of the word gradually slips back, and the conclusions arrived at seem, therefore, quite different from what they would be seen to be if the initial definition had been remembered.

The point is, of course, that, so soon as it is admitted that there are things that exist, it is impossible to avoid recognizing a distinction, to which we may give what name we please, between believing in the existence of something that exists and believing in the existence of something that does not exist. It is common to call the one belief true, the other false. But if, with the pragmatists, we prefer to give a different meaning to the words 'true' and 'false', that does not prevent the distinction commonly called the distinction of 'true' and 'false' from persisting. The pragmatist attempt to ignore this distinction fails, as it seems to me, because a basis of fact cannot be avoided by pragmatism, and this basis of fact demands the *usual* antithesis of 'true' and 'false'. It is hardly to be supposed that pragmatists will admit this conclusion. But it may be hoped that they will tell us in more detail how they propose to avoid it.

Pragmatism, if I have not misunderstood it, is largely a generalization from the procedure of the inductive sciences. In so far as it lays stress upon the importances of induction, I find myself in agreement with it; and as to the nature of induction also, I think it is far more nearly right than are most of the traditional accounts. But on fundamental questions of philosophy I find myself wholly opposed to it, and unable to see that inductive procedure gives any warrant for its conclusions. To make this clear, I will very briefly explain how I conceive the nature and scope of induction.

When we survey our beliefs, we find that we hold different beliefs with very different degrees of conviction. Some—such as the belief that I am sitting in a chair, or that $2+2=4$—can be doubted by few except those who have had a long training in philosophy. Such beliefs are held so firmly that non-philosophers who deny them are put into lunatic asylums. Other beliefs, such as the facts of history, are held rather less firmly, but still in the main without much doubt where they are well authenticated. Beliefs about the future, as that the sun will rise tomorrow and that the trains will run approximately as in Bradshaw, may be held with almost as great conviction as beliefs about the past. Scientific laws are generally believed less firmly, and there is a gradation among them from such as seem nearly certain to such as have only a slight probability in their favour. Philosophical beliefs, finally, will, with most people, take a still lower place, since the opposite beliefs of others can hardly fail to induce doubt. Belief, therefore, is a matter of degree. To speak of belief, disbelief, doubt, and suspense of judgment as the only possibilities is as if, from the writing on the thermometer, we were to suppose that blood heat, summer heat, temperate, and freezing were the only temperatures. There is a continuous gradation in belief, and the more firmly we believe anything, the less willing we are to abandon it in case of conflict.

Besides the degree of our belief, there is another important respect in which a belief may vary, namely, in the extent to which it is *spontaneous* or *derivative*. A belief obtained by inference may be called *derivative*; one not so obtained, *spontaneous*. When we do not need any outside evidence to make us entertain a belief, we may say that what we believe is *obvious*. Our belief in the existence of sensible objects is of this nature: 'seeing is believing', and we demand no further evidence. The same applies to certain logical principles, e.g. that whatever follows from a true proposition must be true. A proposition may be obvious in very varying degrees. For example, in matters of æsthetic taste we have to judge immediately whether a work of art is beautiful or not, but the degree of obviousness involved is probably small, so that we feel no very great confidence in our judgment. Thus our spontaneous beliefs are not necessarily stronger than derivative beliefs. Moreover, few beliefs, if any, are *wholly* spontaneous in an educated man. The more a man has organized his knowledge, the more his beliefs will be interdependent, and the more will obvious truths be reinforced by their connection with other obvious truths. In spite of this fact, however, obviousness remains always the ultimate source of our beliefs; for what is called verification or deduction consists always in being brought into relation with one or more obvious propositions. This process of verification is necessary even for propositions which seem obvious, since it appears on examination that two apparently obvious propositions may be inconsistent, and hence that apparent obviousness is not a sufficient guarantee of truth. We therefore have to subject our beliefs to a process of organization, making groups of such as are mutually consistent, and when two such groups are not consistent with each other, selecting that group which seems to us to contain the most evidence, account being taken both of the degree of obviousness of the propositions it contains and of the number of such propositions. It is as the result of such a process, for example, that we are led, if we are led, to conclude that colours are not objective properties of things. Induction, in a broad sense, may be described as the process of selecting hypotheses which will organize our spontaneous beliefs, preserving as many of them as possible, and interconnecting them by general propositions which, as is said, 'explain' them, i.e. give a ground from which they can be deduced. In this sense, all knowledge is inductive as soon as it is reflective and organized. In any science, there is a greater or less degree of obviousness about many of its propositions: those that are obvious are called *data*; other propositions are only accepted because of their connection with the data. This connection itself may be of two kinds, either that the propositions in question can be deduced from the data, or that the data can be deduced from the propositions in question, and we know of no way of deducing the data without assuming the propositions in question. The latter is the case of working hypotheses, which covers all the general laws of science and all the metaphysics both of common sense and of professed philosophy. It is, apparently, by generalizing the conception of 'working hypothesis' that pragmatism has arisen. But three points seem to me to have been overlooked in this generalization. First, working hypotheses are only a small part of our beliefs, not the whole, as pragmatism seems to think. Secondly, prudent people give only a low degree of belief to working hypotheses; it is therefore a curious procedure to select them as the very types of beliefs in general. Thirdly,

pragmatism seems to confound two very different conceptions of 'working'. When *science* says that a hypothesis works,
it means that from this hypothesis we can deduce a number
of propositions which are verifiable, i.e. obvious under suitable circumstances, and that we cannot deduce any propositions of which the contradictories are verifiable. But when
pragmatism says that a hypothesis works, it means that the
effects of believing it are good, including among the effects
not only the beliefs which we deduce from it, but also the
emotions entailed by it or its perceived consequences, and the
actions to which we are prompted by it or its perceived consequences. This is a totally different conception of 'working',
and one for which the authority of scientific procedure cannot be invoked. I infer, therefore, that induction, rightly
analysed, does not lead us to pragmatism, and that the inductive results which pragmatism takes as the very type of
truth are precisely those among our beliefs which should be
held with most caution and least conviction.

To sum up: while agreeing with the empirical temper of
pragmatism, with its readiness to treat all philosophical
tenets as 'working hypotheses', we cannot agree that when
we say a belief is true we mean that it is a hypothesis which
'works', especially if we mean by this to take account of the
excellence of its effects, and not merely of the truth of its consequences. If, to avoid disputes about words, we agree to
accept the pragmatic definition of the word 'truth', we find
that the belief that A exists may be 'true' even when A does
not exist. This shows that the conclusions arrived at by pragmatism in the sphere of religion do not have the meaning
which they appear to have, and are incapable, when rightly
understood, of yielding us the satisfaction which they promise.
The attempt to get rid of 'fact' turns out to be a failure, and
thus the old notion of truth reappears. And if the pragmatist
states that utility is to be merely a *criterion* of truth, we shall
reply first, that it is not a useful criterion, because it is usually
harder to discover whether a belief is useful than whether it
is true; secondly, that since no *a priori* reason is shown why

truth and utility should always go together, utility can only be shown to be a criterion at all by showing inductively that it accompanies truth in all known instances, which requires that we should already know in many instances what things are true. Finally, therefore, the pragmatist theory of truth is to be condemned on the ground that it does not 'work'.

VI

THE MONISTIC THEORY OF TRUTH[1]

I

In any inquiry into the nature of truth, two questions meet us on the threshold: (1) In what sense, if any, is truth dependent upon mind? (2) Are there many different truths, or is there only *the* Truth? These two questions are largely interconnected, and it is more or less optional whether we begin with the first or with the second. But, on the whole, the second, namely, the question whether we ought to speak of *truths* or of *the Truth*, seems the more fundamental, and the bulk of the present essay will be occupied with this question. The view that truth is one may be called 'logical monism'; it is, of course, closely connected with ontological monism, i.e. the doctrine that Reality is one. The following essay will consist of two parts. In the first I shall state the monistic theory of truth, sketching the philosophy with which it is bound up, and shall then consider certain internal difficulties of this philosophy, which suggests a doubt as to the axioms upon which the philosophy is based. In the second part I shall consider the chief of these axioms, namely, the axiom that relations are always grounded in the natures of their terms, and I shall try to show that there are no reasons in favour of this axiom and strong reasons against it.[2]

'That the truth itself', Mr Joachim says, 'is one, and whole,

[1] The following essay consists of the first two sections of an article entitled 'The Nature of Truth', which appeared in the *Proceedings of the Aristotelian Society*, 1906–7.

[2] I shall throughout often refer to Mr Joachim's book, *The Nature of Truth* (Oxford, 1906), because it gives what seems to me the best recent statement of certain views which I wish to discuss. I shall refer to this book as 'Joachim'.

and complete, and that all thinking and all experience move within its recognition and subject to its manifest authority; this I have never doubted' (p. 178).

This doctrine, which is one of the foundation-stones of monistic idealism, has a sweep which might not be obvious at once. It means that nothing is wholly true except the whole truth, and that what seem to be isolated truths, such as $2+2 =4$, are really only true in the sense that they form part of the system which is the whole truth. And even in this sense isolated truths are only more or less true; for when artificially isolated they are bereft of aspects and relations which make them parts of the whole truth, and are thus altered from what they are in the system. If account were taken of all the relations of a certain partial truth to other partial truths, we should be brought to the whole system of truth, and thus the partial truth from which we started would have developed into the one absolute truth. The truth that a certain partial truth is part of the whole is a partial truth, and thus only partially true; hence we can never say with perfect truth 'this is part of the Truth'. Hence there can be no sense of truth which is completely applicable to a partial truth, because everything that can be said about a partial truth is only a partial truth.

The whole of truth, or indeed whatever is genuinely a whole, is an *organic unity* or *significant whole*, i.e. it is 'such that all its constituent elements reciprocally involve one another, or reciprocally determine one another's being as contributory features in a single concrete meaning' (Joachim, p. 66). This is an obvious consequence of the view that only the whole of truth is quite true; for, if this is the case, the truth about any part of the whole must be the same as the whole truth; thus the complete truth about any part is the same as the complete truth about any other part, since each is the whole of truth.

The position which I have been trying to represent is always considered, by those who hold it, a very difficult one to apprehend; so much so that the word 'crude' has been consecrated to those arguments and philosophies which do not accept this position. As I believe that the more 'crude' a philosophy is, the nearer it comes to being true, I cannot hope to persuade idealists that I have understood their position; I can only assure them that I have done my best.

There are in the above theory—so it seems to me—certain intrinsic difficulties which ought to make us suspicious of the premisses from which it follows. The first of these difficulties —and it is one which is very candidly faced by Mr Joachim —is that, if no partial truth is quite true, it cannot be quite true that no partial truth is quite true; unless indeed the whole of truth is contained in the proposition 'no partial truth is quite true', which is too sceptical a view for the philosophy we are considering. Connected with this is the difficulty that human beings can never know anything quite true, because their knowledge is not of the whole of truth. Thus the philosophy with which the view in question is bound up cannot be quite true, since, if it were, it could not be known to idealists. And it may be that the elements in their knowledge which require correction are just those which are essential to establishing their view of truth; so long as our premisses are more or less faulty, we cannot know that, if corrected, they would give the results we have deduced from them. But this objection—that truth, if it is as alleged, must remain unknowable to us—is met by challenging the distinction between finite minds and Mind. A distinction is necessarily a partial truth; hence, if we distinguish a and b, we are only partly right: in another aspect, a and b are identical. Thus, although in a sense we may distinguish our finite knowledge from absolute knowledge, yet in another sense we may say that our knowledge is only real in so far as it is not finite; for the reality of what is finite is the whole of which it is a constituent. Thus we, so far as we are real, do really know all truth; but only idealists know that they know all truth.

The objections we have just been considering are based upon the difficulty as to what monism means by a *whole*, and in what sense it conceives that a whole has parts. The uninitiated might imagine that a whole is made up of parts, each of which is a genuine constituent of the whole, and is something on its own account. But this view is 'crude'. The parts of a whole are not self-subsistent, and have no being except as parts. We can never enumerate parts a, b, c, . . . of a whole W; for the proposition 'a is part of W' is only a partial truth, and therefore not quite true. Not only is this proposition not quite true, but the past a is not quite real. Thus W is a whole of parts all of which are not quite real. It follows that W is not quite really a whole of parts. If it is not quite true that W has parts, it cannot be quite true that W is a whole. In short, the diversity which modern monism tries to synthesise with identity vanishes, leaving reality wholly without structure or complexity of any kind. For though it is essential to its being a whole that it should have parts, it is essential to its being a *significant* whole that its parts should not quite truly be its parts, since every statement about them, including the statement that they are its parts, must be more or less untrue.

A connected difficulty is the following: In a 'significant whole', each part, since it involves the whole and every other part, is just as complex as the whole; the parts of a part, in turn, are just as complex as the part, and therefore just as complex as the whole. Since, moreover, the whole is constitutive of the nature of each part, just as much as each part is of the whole, we may say that the whole is part of each part. In these circumstances it becomes perfectly arbitrary to say that a is part of W rather than that W is part of a. If we are to say this, we shall have to supplement the monist's notion of whole and part by a more commonplace notion, which I think is really present, though unconsciously, in all monistic thinking; for otherwise the distinction of whole and part evaporates, and with it the entire notion of a 'significant whole'.

Another difficulty of the monistic theory of truth is as to *error*. Every separate proposition, on the monistic theory, expresses a *partial* truth: no proposition expresses something quite true, and none expresses something quite false. Under these circumstances, the distinctive characteristic of error cannot lie in the judgment affirmed, since every possible judgment is partially true and partially false. Mr Joachim, who has considered very carefully the whole question of error, comes to the conclusion—which seems the only possible one for a monistic theory of truth—that the essential characteristic of error is the claim to express truth unqualified (p. 143). He says: 'The erring subject's confident belief in the truth of his knowledge distinctively characterizes error, and converts a partial apprehension of the truth into falsity' (p. 162). Now this view has one great merit, namely, that it makes error consist wholly and solely in rejection of the monistic theory of truth. As long as this theory is accepted, no judgment is an error; as soon as it is rejected, every judgment is an error. But there are some objections to be urged against this comfortable conclusion. If I affirm, with a 'confident belief in the truth of my knowledge', that Bishop Stubbs used to wear episcopal gaiters, that is an error; if a monistic philosopher, remembering that all finite truth is only partially true, affirms that Bishop Stubbs was hanged for murder, that is not an error. Thus it seems plain that Mr Joachim's criterion does not distinguish between right and wrong judgments as ordinarily understood, and that its inability to make such a distinction is a mark of defect. If a jury, for example, has to decide whether a man has committed a crime, Mr Joachim's criterion gives no means of distinguishing between a right and a wrong verdict. If the jury remember the monistic philosophy, either verdict is right; if they forget it, either is wrong. What I wish to make plain is, that there is a sense in which such a proposition as 'A murdered B' is true or false; and that in this sense the proposition in question does not depend, for its truth or falsehood, upon whether it is regarded as a partial truth or not. And this sense, it seems to me, is presupposed in constructing the whole of truth; for the whole of truth is composed of propositions which are true in this sense, since it is impossible to believe that the proposition 'Bishop Stubbs was hanged for murder' is part of the whole of truth.

The adherent of the monistic theory of truth may reply that one who remembers this theory will not assert that

Bishop Stubbs was hanged for murder, since he will realize that such an assertion would clash with known facts, and would be incapable of fitting into the coherent whole of truth. Now it might be enough to reply that the supposed immunity from errors of fact is not secured by the theory that truth is coherence; since, for example, Hegel was mistaken as to the number of the planets. But this would be an inadequate reply. The true reply is, that we are concerned with the question, not how far a belief in the coherence-theory is a *cause* of avoidance of error, but how far this theory is able to explain what we *mean* by error. And the objection to the coherence-theory lies in this, that it presupposes a more usual meaning of truth and falsehood in constructing its coherent whole, and that this more usual meaning, though indispensable to the theory, cannot be explained by means of the theory. The proposition 'Bishop Stubbs was hanged for murder' is, we are told, not coherent with the whole of truth or with experience. But that means, when we examine it, that something is *known* which is inconsistent with this proposition. Thus what is inconsistent with the proposition must be something *true:* it may be perfectly possible to construct a coherent whole of *false* propositions in which 'Bishop Stubbs was hanged for murder' would find a place. In a word, the partial truths of which the whole of truth is composed must be such propositions as would commonly be called true, not such as would commonly be called false; there is no explanation, on the coherence-theory, of the distinction commonly expressed by the words 'true' and 'false', and no evidence that a system of false propositions might not, as in a good novel, be just as coherent as the system which is the whole of truth.

The answer to this possibility of several coherent systems is an appeal to 'experience'. Mr Joachim says (p. 78): 'Truth, we said, was the systematic coherence which characterized a significant whole. And we proceeded to identify a significant whole with "an organized individual experience, self-fulfilling and self-fulfilled". Now there can be one *and only one* such experience: or *only one* significant whole, the significance of which is self-contained in the sense required. For it is *absolute* self-fulfilment, *absolutely* self-contained significance, that is postulated; and nothing short of *absolute* individuality—nothing short of *the* completely whole experience—can satisfy this postulate. And human knowledge—not merely *my* knowledge or *yours*, but the best and fullest knowledge in the world at any stage of its development—is clearly not a significant whole in this ideally complete sense. Hence the truth, which our sketch described, is—*from the point of view of human intelligence*—an Ideal, and an Ideal which can never, *as such*, or in its completeness, be actual as human experience.'

This passage introduces two aspects of the monistic theory which we have not yet considered, namely, its appeal to what it calls 'experience' and its use of the *deus ex machina*. Of these, the first, at least, deserves some discussion.

The distinction between knowing something and the something which we know—between, for example, knowing that the pavements are wet and the actual wetness of the pavements—cannot be accepted by the monistic theory of truth, for this theory, as we said, is compelled to regard *all* distinctions as only partially valid. According to this theory, the wetness of the pavements and my knowledge of this wetness, like every other pair of apparently distinct objects, really exhibit a combination of identity in difference. Thus knowledge is in a sense different from its object, but is also in a sense identical with its object. The sense in which it is identical may be further defined as whatever sense is necessary to refute those who reject the monistic theory of truth.

I will not now consider the main question of the dependence of truth upon experience, which cannot well be discussed except in connection with the theory of relations. I am content for the present to point out an ambiguity in the notion of 'experience'. The proposition 'Bishop Stubbs was hanged for murder' consists of parts given in experience, and put together in a manner which, in other cases, is unfortunately also given in experience. And it is possible to apprehend the proposition, so that in one sense the proposition can be experienced. That is to say, we can have an experience which consists of realizing what the proposition is: we can see a picture of Bishop Stubbs dangling from the gallows. Such are the experiences in novel-reading: we do not *believe* what we read, we merely apprehend it. Thus experience may consist in merely apprehending, not in believing.[1] When we apprehend the proposition 'Bishop Stubbs was hanged for murder', this proposition is, in a sense, a part of our experience; but in another sense, which is that relevant in constructing the whole of truth, we do not experience this proposition, since we are not led to believe it. This distinction shows that experience, in the sense required by Mr Joachim, consists of apprehension of *truth*, and that there is much apprehension which, though experience in one sense, is experience in a sense in which what is false can also be experienced.[2] Thus here, again, *experience*, as used in establishing the monistic theory of truth, is a notion involving a conception of truth other than that which the monistic theory declares to be alone legitimate. For experience is either no help towards constructing the whole of truth, or it is apprehension of the *truth* of single propositions, which are true in a sense in which their contradictories are not true. But this conclusion, if sound, is fatal to the monistic theory of truth.

As for the *deus ex machina*, the ideal experience in which the whole of truth is actualized, I will merely observe that he is in general somewhat discredited, and that idealists themselves are rather ashamed of him, as appears by the fact that they never mention him when they can help it, and that when they do, they introduce him with apologetic words, such as 'what is true *in the end*'—as though what is true 'in the end' were anything different from what is true.

We have thus the following objections to the monistic theory of truth: (1) If no partial truth is quite true, this must

---

[1] Cf. Meinong, *Ueber Annahmen* (Leipzig, 1902), *passim*.

[2] This distinction is connected with the question of Floating Ideas, discussed by Mr Bradley in *Mind*, N.S., No. 60. He argues that the distinction between the real and the imaginary is not absolute, but his argument explicitly assumes what I have called the 'axiom of internal relations'. Cf., e.g., pp. 457–61.

apply to the partial truths which embody the monistic philosophy. But if these are not quite true, any deductions we may make from them may depend upon their false aspect rather than their true one, and may therefore be erroneous. (2) It is a consequence of the monistic theory that the parts of a whole are not really its parts. Hence there cannot be any genuine whole on this theory, since nothing can be really a whole unless it really has parts. (3) The theory is unable to explain in what sense one partial judgment is said to be true and another false, though both are equally partial. (4) In order to prove that there can be only one coherent whole, the theory is compelled to appeal to 'experience', which must consist in knowing particular truths, and thus requires a notion of truth that the monistic theory cannot admit.

But each of these arguments is of the nature of a *reductio ad absurdum*. We must now turn to what I believe to be the fundamental assumption of the whole monistic theory, namely, its doctrine as to relations. If we can show that this doctrine is groundless and untenable, we shall thereby complete the refutation of the monistic theory.

II

The doctrines we have been considering may all be deduced from one central logical doctrine, which may be expressed thus: 'Every relation is grounded in the natures of the related terms.' Let us call this the *axiom of internal relations*. If this axiom holds, the fact that two objects have a certain relation implies complexity in each of the two objects, i.e. it implies something in the 'natures' of the two objects, in virtue of which they have the relation in question. According to the opposite view, which is the one that I advocate, there are such facts as that one object has a certain relation to another, and such facts cannot in general be reduced to, or inferred from, a fact about the one object only together with a fact about the other object only: they do not imply that the two objects have any complexity, or any *intrinsic* property distinguishing them from two objects which do not have the relation in question.

Before examining the arguments for and against the axiom of internal relations, let us consider some of its consequences. It follows at once from this axiom that the whole of reality or of truth must be a significant whole in Mr Joachim's sense. For each part will have a nature which exhibits its relations to every other part and to the whole; hence, if the nature of any one part were completely known, the nature of the whole and of every other part would also be completely known; while conversely, if the nature of the whole were completely known, that would involve knowledge of its relations to each part, and therefore of the relations of each part to each other part, and therefore of the nature of each part. It is also evident that, if reality or truth is a significant whole in Mr Joachim's sense, the axiom of internal relations must be true. Hence the axiom is equivalent to the monistic theory of truth.

Further, assuming that we are not to distinguish between a thing and its 'nature', it follows from the axiom that nothing can be considered quite truly except in relation to the whole. For if we consider 'A is related to B', the A and the B are also related to everything else, and to say what the A and the B are would involve referring to everything else in the universe. When we consider merely that part of A's nature in virtue of which A is related to B, we are said to be considering A *qua* related to B; but this is an abstract and only partially true way of considering A, for A's nature, which is the same thing as A, contains the grounds of its relations to everything else as well as to B. Thus nothing quite true can be said about A short of taking account of the whole universe; and then what is said about A will be the same as what would be said about anything else, since the natures of different things must, like those of Leibniz's monads, all express the same system of relations.

Let us now consider more closely the meaning of the axiom of internal relations and the grounds for and against it. We have, to begin with, two possible meanings, according as it is held that every relation is really *constituted* by the natures of the terms or of the whole which they compose, or merely that every relation has a *ground* in these natures. I do not observe that idealists distinguish these two meanings; indeed, speaking generally, they tend to identify a proposition with its consequences,[1] thus embodying one of the distinctive tenets of pragmatism. The distinction of the two meanings is, however, less important than it would otherwise be, owing to the fact that both meanings lead, as we shall see, to the view that there are no relations at all.

The axiom of internal relations in either form involves, as Mr Bradley has justly urged,[2] the conclusion that there are no relations and that there are not many things, but only one thing. (Idealists would add: *in the end*. But that only means that the consequence is one which it is often convenient to forget.) This conclusion is reached by considering the relation of diversity. For if there really are two things, A and B, which are diverse, it is impossible to reduce this diversity wholly to adjectives of A and B. It will be necessary that A and B should have *different* adjectives, and the diversity of these adjectives cannot, on pain of an endless regress, be interpreted as *meaning* that they in turn have different adjectives. For if we say that A and B differ when A has the adjective 'different from B' and B has the adjective 'different from A', we must suppose that these two adjectives differ. Then 'different from A' must have the adjective 'different from "different from B" ', which must differ from 'different from "different from A" ', and so on *ad infinitum*. We cannot take 'different from B' as an adjective requiring no further reduction, since we must ask what is meant by 'different' in this phrase, which, as it stands, derives an adjective from a relation, not a relation from an adjective. Thus, if there is to be any diversity, there

---

[1] Cf., e.g., Joachim, p. 108.

[2] Cf. *Appearance and Reality*, 1st ed., p. 519: 'Reality is one. It must be single, because plurality, taken as real, contradicts itself. Plurality implies relations, and, through its relations, it unwillingly asserts always a superior unity.'

must be a diversity not reducible to difference of adjectives, i.e. not grounded in the 'natures' of the diverse terms. Consequently, if the axiom of internal relations is true, it follows that there is no diversity, and that there is only one thing. Thus the axiom of internal relations is equivalent to the assumption of ontological monism and to the denial that there are any relations. Wherever we seem to have a relation, this is really an adjective of the whole composed of the terms of the supposed relation.

The axiom of internal relations is thus equivalent to the assumption that every proposition has one subject and one predicate. For a proposition which asserts a relation must always be reduced to a subject-predicate proposition concerning the whole composed of the terms of the relation. Proceeding in this way to larger and larger wholes, we gradually correct our first crude abstract judgments, and approximate more and more to the one truth about the whole. The one final and complete truth must consist of a proposition with one subject, namely the whole, and one predicate. But since this involves distinguishing subject from predicate, as though they could be diverse, even this is not quite true. The best we can say of it is, that it is not '*intellectually* corrigible', i.e. it is as true as any truth can be; but even absolute truth persists in being not quite true.[1]

If we ask ourselves what are the grounds in favour of the axiom of internal relations, we are left in doubt by those who believe in it. Mr Joachim, for example, assumes it throughout, and advances no argument in its favour.[2] So far as one can discover the grounds, they seem to be two, though these are perhaps really indistinguishable. There is first the law of

[1] Cf. *Appearance and Reality*, 1st ed., p. 544: 'Even absolute truth in the end seems thus to turn out to be erroneous. And it must be admitted that, in the end, no possible truth is quite true. It is a partial and inadequate translation of that which it professes to give bodily. And this internal discrepancy belongs irremovably to truth's proper character. Still, the difference, drawn between absolute and finite truth, must none the less be upheld. For the former, in a word, is not *intellectually* corrigible.'

[2] See *Mind*, October 1906, pp. 530–1.

sufficient reason, according to which nothing can be just a brute fact, but must have some reason for being thus and not otherwise.[1] Secondly, there is the fact that, if two terms have a certain relation, they cannot but have it, and if they did not have it they would be different; which seems to show that there is something in the terms themselves which leads to their being related as they are.

(1) The law of sufficient reason is hard to formulate precisely. It cannot merely mean that every true proposition is logically deducible from some other true proposition, for this is an obvious truth which does not yield the consequences demanded of the law. For example, $2+2=4$ can be deduced from $4+4=8$, but it would be absurd to regard $4+4=8$ as a reason for $2+2=4$. The *reason* for a proposition is always expected to be one or more *simpler* propositions. Thus the law of sufficient reason should mean that every proposition can be deduced from simpler propositions. This seems obviously false, but in any case it cannot be relevant in considering idealism, which holds propositions to be less and less true the simpler they are, so that it would be absurd to insist on starting from simple propositions. I conclude, therefore, that, if any form of the law of sufficient reason is relevant, it is rather to be discovered by examining the second of the grounds in favour of the axiom of internal relations, namely, that related terms cannot but be related as they are.

(2) The force of this argument depends in the main, I think, upon a fallacious form of statement. 'If A and B are related in a certain way', it may be said, 'you must admit that if they were not so related they would be other than they are, and that consequently there must be something in them which is essential to their being related as they are.' Now if two terms are related in a certain way, it follows that, if they were not so related, every imaginable consequence would ensue.

---

[1] Cf. *Appearance and Reality*, 2nd ed., p. 575: 'If the terms from their own inner nature do not enter into the relation, then, so far as they are concerned, they seem related for no reason at all, and, so far as they are concerned, the relation seems arbitrarily made.' Cf. also p. 577.

For, if they are so related, the hypothesis that they are not so related is false, and from a false hypothesis anything can be deduced. Thus the above form of statement must be altered. We may say: 'If A and B are related in a certain way, then anything not so related must be other than A and B, hence, etc.' But this only proves that what is not related as A and B are must be *numerically* diverse from A or B; it will not prove difference of adjectives, unless we assume the axiom of internal relations. Hence the argument has only a rhetorical force, and cannot prove its conclusion without a vicious circle.

It remains to ask whether there are any grounds *against* the axiom of internal relations. The first argument that naturally occurs to an opponent of this axiom is the difficulty of actually carrying it out. We have had one instance of this already as regards diversity: in many other instances the difficulty is even more obvious. Suppose, for example, that one volume is greater than another. We may reduce the relation 'greater than' between the volumes to adjectives of the volumes, by saying that one is of such and such a size and the other of such and such another size. But then the one size must be greater than the other size. If we try to reduce this new relation to adjectives of the two sizes, the adjectives must still have a relation corresponding to 'greater than', and so on. Hence we cannot, without an endless regress, refuse to admit that sooner or later we come to a relation not reducible to adjectives of the related terms. This argument applies especially to all *asymmetrical* relations, i.e. to such as, when they hold between A and B, do not hold between B and A.[1]

A more searching argument against the axiom of internal relations is derived from a consideration of what is meant by the 'nature' of a term. Is this the same as the term itself, or is it different? If it is different, it must be related to the term, and the relation of a term to its nature cannot without an endless regress be reduced to something other than a relation. Thus if the axiom is to be adhered to, we must suppose that a

[1] The argument which is merely indicated above is set forth fully in my *Principles of Mathematics*, §§ 212–16.

term is not other than its nature. In that case, every true proposition attributing a predicate to a subject is purely analytic, since the subject is its own whole nature, and the predicate is part of that nature. But in that case, what is the bond that unites predicates into predicates of one subject? Any casual collection of predicates might be supposed to compose a subject, if subjects are not other than the system of their own predicates. If the 'nature' of a term is to consist of predicates, and at the same time to be the same as the term itself, it seems impossible to understand what we mean when we ask whether S has the predicate P. For this cannot mean: 'Is P one of the predicates enumerated in explaining what we mean by S?' and it is hard to see what else, on the view in question, it could mean. We cannot attempt to introduce a relation of *coherence* between predicates, in virtue of which they may be called predicates of one subject; for this would base predication upon a relation, instead of reducing relations to predications. Thus we get into equal difficulties whether we affirm or deny that a subject is other than its 'nature'.[1]

Again, the axiom of internal relation is incompatible with all complexity. For this axiom leads, as we saw, to a rigid monism. There is only one thing and only one proposition. The one proposition (which is not merely the only *true* proposition, but the *only* proposition) attributes a predicate to the one subject. But this one proposition is not quite true, because it involves distinguishing the predicate from the subject. But then arises the difficulty: if predication involves difference of the predicate from the subject, and if the one predicate is *not* distinct from the one subject, there cannot, even, one would suppose, be a *false* proposition attributing the one predicate to the one subject. We shall have to suppose, therefore, that predication does not involve difference of the predicate from the subject, and that the one predicate is identical with the one subject. But it is essential to the philosophy we are examining to deny absolute identity and

[1] On this subject cf. my *Philosophy of Leibniz*, §§ 21, 24, 25.

retain 'identity in difference'. The apparent multiplicity of the real world is otherwise inexplicable. The difficulty is that 'identity in difference' is impossible, if we adhere to strict monism. For 'identity in difference' involves many partial truths, which combine, by a kind of mutual give and take, into the one whole of truth. But the partial truths, in a strict monism, are not merely not quite true: they do not subsist at all. If there were such propositions, whether true or false, that would give plurality. In short, the whole conception of 'identity in difference' is incompatible with the axiom of internal relations; yet without this conception monism can give no account of the world, which suddenly collapses like an opera-hat. I conclude that the axiom is false, and that those parts of idealism which depend upon it are therefore groundless.

There would seem, therefore, to be reasons against the axiom that relations are necessarily grounded in the 'nature' of their terms or of the whole composed of the terms, and there would seem to be no reason in favour of this axiom. When the axiom is rejected, it becomes meaningless to speak of the 'nature' of the terms of a relation: relatedness is no longer a proof of complexity, a given relation may hold between many different pairs of terms, and a given term may have many different relations to different terms. 'Identity in difference' disappears: there is identity and there is difference, and complexes may have some elements identical and some different, but we are no longer obliged to say of any pair of objects that may be mentioned that they are both identical and different—'in a sense', this 'sense' being something which it is vitally necessary to leave undefined. We thus get a world of many things, with relations which are not to be deduced from a supposed 'nature' or scholastic essence of the related things. In this world, whatever is complex is composed of related simple things, and analysis is no longer confronted at every step by an endless regress. Assuming this kind of world, it remains to ask what we are to say concerning the nature of truth. This question is considered in the following essay.

VII

ON THE NATURE OF TRUTH AND FALSEHOOD

The question 'What is Truth?' is one which may be understood in several different ways, and before beginning our search for an answer, it will be well to be quite clear as to the sense in which we are asking the question. We may mean to ask what things are true: is science true? is revealed religion true? and so on. But before we can answer such questions as these, we ought to be able to say what these questions *mean*: what is it, exactly, that we are asking when we say, 'is science true?' It is this preliminary question that I wish to discuss. The question whether this or that is true is to be settled, if at all, by considerations concerning this or that, not by general considerations as to what 'truth' means; but those who ask the question presumably have in their minds already some idea as to what 'truth' means, otherwise the question and its answer could have no definite meaning to them.

When, however, we have agreed that the question we are concerned with is 'What does "truth" mean?' we have by no means come to an end of possible ambiguities. There is the question 'How is the word "truth" properly used?' This is a question for the dictionary, not for philosophy. Moreover, the word has some perfectly proper uses which are obviously irrelevant to our inquiry: a 'true' man, a 'true' poet, are 'true' in a different sense from that with which we are concerned. Again, there is the question 'What do people usually have in mind when they use the word "truth"?' This question comes nearer to the question we have to ask, but is still different from it. The question what idea people have when they use a word is a question of psychology; moreover, there is very little in common between the ideas which two different people in fact attach to the same word, though there would often be more agreement as to the ideas which they would consider it proper to attach to the word.

The question we have to discuss may be explained by pointing out that, in the case of such a word as 'truth', we all feel that some fundamental concept, of great philosophical importance, is involved, though it is difficult to be clear as to what this concept is. What we wish to do is to detach this concept from the mass of irrelevancies in which, when we use it, it is normally embedded, and to bring clearly before the mind the abstract opposition upon which our distinction of true and false depends. The process to be gone through is essentially one of analysis: we have various complex and more or less confused beliefs about the true and the false, and we have to reduce these to forms which are simple and clear, without causing any avoidable conflict between our initial complex and confused beliefs and our final simple and clear assertions. These final assertions are to be tested partly by their intrinsic evidence, partly by their power of accounting for the 'data'; and the 'data', in such a problem, are the complex and confused beliefs with which we start. These beliefs must necessarily suffer a change in becoming clear, but the change should not be greater than is warranted by their initial confusion.

Although the question what things are true rather than false does not form part of our inquiry, yet it will be useful to consider for a moment the nature of the things to which we attribute either truth or falsehood. Broadly speaking, the things that are true or false, in the sense with which we are concerned, are statements, and beliefs or judgments.[1] When, for example, we see the sun shining, the sun itself is not 'true', but the judgment 'the sun is shining' is true. The truth or falsehood of statements can be defined in terms of the truth or falsehoods of beliefs. A statement is true when a person who

[1] I shall use the words 'belief' and 'judgment' as synonyms.

believes it believes truly, and false when a person who believes it believes falsely. Thus in considering the nature of truth we may confine ourselves to the truth of beliefs, since the truth of statements is a notion derived from that of beliefs. The question we have to discuss is therefore: What is the difference between a true belief and a false belief? By this I mean, What is the difference which actually *constitutes* the truth or falsehood of a belief? I am not asking for what is called a *criterion* of truth, i.e. for some quality, other than truth, which belongs to whatever is true and to nothing else. This distinction between the *nature* of truth and a *criterion* of truth is important, and has not always been sufficiently emphasized by philosophers. A criterion is a sort of trade-mark, i.e some comparatively obvious characteristic which is a guarantee of genuineness. 'None genuine without the label': thus the label is what assures us that such and such a firm made the article. But when we say that such and such a firm made the article we do not *mean* that the article has the right label; thus there is a difference between meaning and criterion. Indeed, it is just this difference which makes a criterion useful. Now I do not believe that truth has, universally, any such trade-mark: I do not believe that there is any one label by which we can always know that a judgment is true rather than false. But this is not the question which I wish to discuss: I wish to discuss what truth and falsehood actually are, not what extraneous marks they have by which we can recognize them.

The first point upon which it is important to be clear is the relation of truth and falsehood to the mind. If we were right in saying that the things that are true or false are always judgments, then it is plain that there can be no truth or falsehood unless there are minds to judge. Nevertheless it is plain, also, that the truth or falsehood of a given judgment depends in no way upon the person judging, but solely upon the facts about which he judges. If I judge that Charles I died in his bed, I judge falsely, not because of anything to do with me, but because in fact he did not die in his bed. Similarly, if I judge that he died on the scaffold, I judge truly, because of an event which in fact occurred 260 years ago. Thus the truth or false-hood of a judgment always has an objective ground, and it is natural to ask whether there are not objective truths and falsehoods which are the objects, respectively, of true and false judgments. As regards truths, this view is highly plaus-ible. But as regards falsehoods, it is the very reverse of plaus-ible; yet, as we shall see, it is hard to maintain it with regard to truths without being forced to maintain it also as regards falsehoods.

In all cognitive acts, such as believing, doubting, disbeliev-ing, apprehending, perceiving, imagining, the mind has objects other than itself to which it stands in some one of these various relations. In such a case as perception this is sufficiently obvious: the thing perceived is necessarily some-thing different from the act of perceiving it, and the perceiv-ing is a relation between the person perceiving and the thing perceived. The same thing holds, though less obviously, with regard to imagination. If I imagine, say, a certain colour, the colour is an object before my mind just as truly as if I per-ceived the colour, though the relation to my mind is different from what it would be if I perceived the colour, and does not lead me to suppose that the colour exists in the place where I imagine it. Judgments, also, consist of relations of the mind to objects. But here a distinction has to be made between two different theories as to the relation which constitutes judg-ment. If I judge (say) that Charles I died on the scaffold, is that a relation between me and a single 'fact', namely, Charles I's death on the scaffold, or 'that Charles I died on the scaffold', or is it a relation between me and Charles I and dying and the scaffold? We shall find that the possibility of false judgments compels us to adopt the latter view. But let us first examine the view that a judgment has a single object.

If every judgment, whether true or false, consists in a certain relation, called 'judging' or 'believing', to a single object, which is what we judge or believe, then the distinction of true and false as applied to judgments is derivative from the distinction of true and false as applied to the objects of judgments. Assuming that there are such objects, let us, following Meinong, give them the name 'Objectives'. Then every judgment has an objective, and true judgments have true objectives, while false judgments have false objectives. Thus the question of the meaning of truth and falsehood will have to be considered first with regard to objectives, and we shall have to find some way of dividing objectives into those that are true and those that are false. In this, however, there is great difficulty. So long as we only consider true judgments, the view that they have objectives is plausible: the actual event which we describe as 'Charles I's death on the scaffold' may be regarded as the objective of the judgment 'Charles I died on the scaffold'. But what is the objective of the judgment 'Charles I died in his bed'? There was no event such as 'Charles I's death in his bed'. To say that there ever was such a thing as 'Charles I's death in his bed' is merely another way of saying that Charles I died in his bed. Thus, if there is an objective, it must be something other than 'Charles I's death in his bed'. We may take it to be 'that Charles I died in his bed'. We shall then have to say the same of true judgments: the objective of 'Charles I died on the scaffold' will be 'that Charles I died on the scaffold'.

To this view there are, however, two objections. The first is that it is difficult to believe that there are such objects as 'that Charles I died in his bed', or even 'that Charles I died on the scaffold'. It seems evident that the phrase 'that so and so' has no complete meaning by itself, which would enable it to denote a definite object as (e.g.) the word 'Socrates' does. We feel that the phrase 'that so and so' is essentially incomplete, and only acquires full significance when words are added so as to express a judgment, e.g. 'I believe that so and so', 'I deny that so and so', 'I hope that so and so'. Thus, if we can avoid regarding 'that so and so' as an independent entity, we shall escape a paradox. This argument is not decisive, but it must be allowed a certain weight. The second objection is more fatal, and more germane to the consideration of truth and falsehood. If we allow that all judgments have objectives, we shall have to allow that there are objectives which are false. Thus there will be in the world entities, not dependent upon the existence of judgments, which can be described as objective falsehoods. This is in itself almost incredible: we feel that there could be no falsehood if there were no minds to make mistakes. But it has the further drawback that it leaves the difference between truth and falsehood quite inexplicable. We feel that when we judge truly some entity 'corresponding' in some way to our judgment is to be found outside our judgment, while when we judge falsely there is no such 'corresponding' entity. It is true we cannot take as this entity simply the grammatical subject of our judgment: if we judge, e.g., 'Homer did not exist', it is obvious that Homer is not the entity which is to be found if our judgment is true, but not if it is false. Nevertheless it is difficult to abandon the view that, in some way, the truth or falsehood of a judgment depends upon the presence or absence of a 'corresponding' entity of some sort. And if we do abandon this view, and adhere to the opinion that there are both true and false objectives, we shall be compelled to regard it as an ultimate and not further explicable fact that objectives are of two sorts, the true and the false. This view, though not logically impossible, is unsatisfactory, and we shall do better, if we can, to find some view which leaves the difference between truth and falsehood less of a mystery.

It might be thought that we could say simply that true judgments have objectives while false ones do not. With a new definition of objectives this view might become tenable, but it is not tenable so long as we hold to the view that judgment actually is a relation of the mind to an objective. For this view compels us, since there certainly are false judgments, and a relation cannot be a relation to nothing, to admit that false judgments as well as true ones have objectives. We must therefore abandon the view that judgments consist in a relation to a single object. We cannot maintain this view with regard to true judgments while rejecting it with regard to false ones, for that would make an intrinsic difference between true and false judgments, and enable us (what is obviously impossible) to discover the truth or falsehood of a judgment merely by examining the intrinsic nature of the judgment. Thus we must turn to the theory that *no* judgment consists in a relation to a single object.

The difficulty of the view we have been hitherto considering was that it compelled us either to admit objective falsehoods, or to admit that when we judge falsely there is nothing that we are judging. The way out of the difficulty consists in maintaining that, whether we judge truly or whether we judge falsely, there is no one thing that we are judging. When we judge that Charles I died on the scaffold, we have before us, not one object, but several objects, namely, Charles I and dying and the scaffold. Similarly, when we judge that Charles I died in his bed, we have before us the objects Charles I, dying, and his bed. These objects are not fictions: they are just as good as the objects of the true judgment. We therefore escape the necessity of admitting objective falsehoods, or of admitting that in judging falsely we have nothing before the mind. Thus in this view judgment is a relation of the mind to several other terms: when these other terms have *inter se* a 'corresponding' relation, the judgment is true; when not, it is false. This view, which I believe to be the correct one, must now be further expanded and explained.

In saying that judgment is a relation of the mind to several things, e.g. to Charles I and the scaffold and dying, I do not mean that the mind has a certain relation to Charles I and also has this relation to the scaffold and also has it to dying. I do not, however, wish to deny that, when we are judging, we have *a* relation to each of the constituents of our judgment separately, for it would seem that we must be in some way conscious of these constituents, so that during any judgment we must have, to each constituent of the judgment, that relation which we may call 'being conscious of it'. This is a very important fact, but it does not give the essence of judgment. Nothing that concerns Charles I and dying and the scaffold separately and severally will give the judgment 'Charles I died on the scaffold'. In order to obtain this judgment, we must have one single unity of the mind and Charles I and dying and the scaffold, i.e. we must have, not several instances of a relation between two terms, but one instance of a relation between more than two terms. Such relations, though familiar to mathematicians, have been unduly ignored by philosophers. Since they appear to me to give the key to many puzzles about truth, I shall make a short digression to show that they are common and ought to be familiar.

One of the commonest ways in which relations between more than two terms occur is in propositions about what happened at some particular time. Take such a proposition as 'A loved B in May and hated him in June', and let us suppose this to be true. Then we cannot say that, apart from dates, A has to B either the relation of loving or that of hating. This necessity for a date does not arise with *all* ordinary relationships; for example, if A is the brother of B, no date is required: the relationship holds always or never, or (more strictly) holds or does not hold without regard to time. But love and hate are 'time's fool': they are not relations which hold without regard to date. 'A loved B in May' is a relation, not between A and B simply, but between A and B and May.[1] This relation between A and B and May cannot be analysed into relations between A and B, A and May, B and May: it is a single unity. It is partly the failure to perceive that the date is one of the terms in such relations which has caused such difficulty in the philosophy of time and change.

As another illustration, take the relation of jealousy. Time comes in here exactly as it did with love and hate, but we will for the moment ignore time, because the point to be noticed about jealousy is that it involves three people. The simplest

[1] I do not want to assume any theory as to the nature of time: 'May' can be interpreted as the reader likes. The statement in the text may then have to be made a little more complicated, but the necessity for a relation of more than two terms will remain.

possible proposition asserting jealousy is such as 'A is jealous of B's love for C', or 'A is jealous of B on account of C'. It might be thought that 'B's love for C' was one term, and A the other term. But this interpretation will not apply to cases of mistaken jealousy: if A is Othello, there is no such thing as 'B's love for C'. Thus this interpretation is impossible, and we are compelled to regard jealousy as a relation of three persons, i.e. as having for its unit a relation which is what we may call 'triangular'. If we further take into account the necessity for a date, the relation becomes 'quadrangular', i.e. the simplest possible proposition involving the relation will be one which concerns four terms, namely, three people and a date.

We will give the name '*multiple* relations' to such as require more than two terms. Thus a relation is 'multiple' if the simplest propositions in which it occurs are propositions involving more than two terms (not counting the relation). From what has been said it is obvious that multiple relations are common, and that many matters cannot be understood without their help. Relations which have only two terms we shall call 'dual relations'.

The theory of judgment which I am advocating is, that judgment is not a dual relation of the mind to a single objective, but a multiple relation of the mind to the various other terms with which the judgment is concerned. Thus if I judge that A loves B, that is not a relation of me to 'A's love for B', but a relation between me and A and love and B. If it were a relation of me to 'A's love for B', it would be impossible unless there were such a thing as 'A's love for B', i.e. unless A loved B, i.e. unless the judgment were true; but in fact false judgments are possible. When the judgment is taken as a relation between me and A and love and B, the mere fact that the judgment occurs does not involve any relation between its objects A and love and B; thus the possibility of false judgments is fully allowed for. When the judgment is true, A loves B; thus *in this case* there *is* a relation between the objects of the judgment. We may therefore state the difference between truth and falsehood as follows: Every judgment is a relation of a mind to several objects, one of which is a relation; the judgment is *true* when the relation which is one of the objects relates the other objects, otherwise it is false. Thus in the above illustration, love, which is a relation, is one of the objects of the judgment, and the judgment is true if love relates A and B. The above statement requires certain additions which will be made later; for the present, it is to be taken as a first approximation.

One of the merits of the above theory is that it explains the difference between judgment and perception, and the reason why perception is not liable to error as judgment is. When we were considering the theory that judgment is a dual relation of the mind to a single objective, we found that so far as true judgments were concerned this theory worked admirably, but that it would not account for false judgments. Now this difficulty will not apply against a corresponding theory of perception. It is true that there are cases where perception *appears* to be at fault, such as dreams and hallucinations. But I believe that in all these cases the perception itself is correct, and what is wrong is a judgment based upon the perception. It would take us too far from our subject to develop this theme, which requires a discussion of the relation between sense-data (i.e. the things we immediately perceive) and what we may call physical reality, i.e. what is there independently of us and our perceptions. Assuming the result of this discussion, I shall take it as agreed that perception, as opposed to judgment, is never in error, i.e. that, whenever we perceive anything, what we perceive exists, at least so long as we are perceiving it.

If the infallibility of perception is admitted, we may apply to perception the theory of the single objective which we found inapplicable to judgment. Take, for example, such a case as spatial relations. Suppose I see simultaneously on my table a knife and a book, the knife being to the left of the book. Perception presents me with a complex object, consisting of the knife and the book in certain relative positions (as well as other objects, which we may ignore). If I attend to this complex object and analyse it, I can arrive at the judgment 'the knife is to the left of the book'. Here the knife and the book and their spatial relation are severally before my mind; but in the perception I had the single whole 'knife-to-left-of-book'. Thus in perception I perceive a single complex object, while in a judgment based upon the perception I have the parts of the complex object separately though simultaneously before me. In order to perceive a complex object, such as 'knife-to-left-of-book', there must be such an object, since otherwise my perception would have no object, i.e. there would not be any perceiving, since the relation of perception requires the two terms, the perceiver and the thing perceived. But if there is such an object as 'knife-to-left-of-book', then the knife must be to the left of the book; hence the judgment 'the knife is to the left of the book' must be true. Thus any judgment of perception, i.e. any judgment derived immediately from perception by mere analysis, must be true. (This does not enable us, in any given case, to be quite certain that such and such a judgment is true, since we may inadvertently have failed merely to analyse what was given in perception.) We see that in the case of the judgment of perception there is, corresponding to the judgment, a certain complex object which is perceived, as one complex, in the perception upon which the judgment is based. It is because there is such a complex object that the judgment is true. This complex object, in the cases where it is perceived, is the objective of the perception. Where it is not perceived, it is still the necessary and sufficient condition of the truth of the judgment. There was such a complex event as 'Charles I's death on the scaffold'; hence the judgment 'Charles I died on the scaffold' is true. There never was such a complex event as 'Charles I's death in his bed'; hence 'Charles I died in his bed' is false. If A loves B, there is such a complex object as 'A's love for B', and vice versa; thus the existence of this complex object gives the condition for the truth of the judgment 'A loves B'. And the same holds in all other cases.

We may now attempt an exact account of the 'correspondence' which constitutes truth. Let us take the judgment 'A loves B'. This consists of a relation of the person judging to A and love and B, i.e. to the two terms A and B and the relation 'love'. But the judgment is not the same as the judgment 'B loves A'; thus the relation must not be abstractly before the mind, but must be before it as proceeding from A to B rather than from B to A. The 'corresponding' complex object which is required to make our judgment true consists of A related to B by the relation which was before us in our judgment. We may distinguish two 'senses' of a relation according as it goes from A to B or from B to A. Then the relation as it enters into the judgment must have a 'sense', and in the corresponding complex it must have the same 'sense'. Thus the judgment that two terms have a certain relation R is a relation of the mind to the two terms and the relation R with the appropriate sense: the 'corresponding' complex consists of the two terms related by the relation R with the same sense. The judgment is true when there is such a complex, and false when there is not. The same account, *mutatis mutandis*, will apply to any other judgment. This gives the definition of truth and falsehood.

We see that, according to the above account, truth and falsehood are primarily properties of judgments, and therefore there would be no truth or falsehood if there were no minds. Nevertheless, the truth or falsehood of a given judgment does not depend upon the person making it or the time when it is made, since the 'corresponding' complex, upon which its truth or falsehood depends, does not contain the person judging as a constituent (except, of course, when the judgment happens to be about oneself). Thus the mixture of dependence upon mind and independence of mind, which we noticed as a characteristic of truth, is fully preserved by our theory.

The questions what things are true and what false, whether we know anything, and if so, how we come to know it, are subsequent to the question 'What is truth?' and except briefly in the case of the judgment of perception, I have avoided such questions in the above discussion, not because they are of less interest, but in order to avoid confusing the issue. It is one of the reasons for the slow progress of philosophy that its fundamental questions are not, to most people, the most interesting, and therefore there is a tendency to hurry on before the foundations are secure. In order to check this tendency, it is necessary to isolate the fundamental questions, and consider them without too much regard to the later developments; and this is what, in respect of one such question, I have tried to do in the foregoing pages.